Cambridge Preliminary English Test 5

WITH ANSWERS

Examination papers from University of Cambridge ESOL Examinations

CAMBRIDGE
UNIVERSITY PRESS

Langcage Pack
(1 Book + 2 CDS) PET

B1
CAM
Ex

CAMBRIDGE UNIVERSITY PRESS
Cambridge, New York, Melbourne, Madrid, Cape Town, Singapore, São Paulo, Delhi

Cambridge University Press
The Edinburgh Building, Cambridge CB2 8RU, UK

www.cambridge.org
Information on this title: www.cambridge.org/9780521714389

© Cambridge University Press 2008

First published 2008
4th printing 2009

Printed in the United Kingdom at the University Press, Cambridge

A catalogue record for this publication is available from the British Library

ISBN 978-0-521-71438-9   Student's Book with answers
ISBN 978-0-521-71437-2   Student's Book
ISBN 978-0-521-71440-2   Audio CDs (2)
ISBN 978-0-521-71439-6   Self-study Pack (Student's Book with answers and Audio CDs (2))

Contents

A Guide to PET

The PET examination is part of a group of examinations developed by Cambridge ESOL called the Cambridge Main Suite. The Main Suite consists of five examinations which have similar characteristics but are designed for different levels of English language ability. Within the five levels, PET Is at Level B1 (Threshold) in the *Council of Europe's Common European Framework of Reference for Languages: Learning, teaching, assessment*. It has also been accredited by the Qualifications and Curriculum Authority in the UK as an Entry Level 3 ESOL certificate in the National Qualifications Framework.

Examination	Council of Europe Framework Level	UK National Qualifications Framework Level
CPE Certificate of Proficiency in English	C2	3
CAE Certificate in Advanced English	C1	2
FCE First Certificate in English	B2	1
PET Preliminary English Test	B1	Entry 3
KET Key English Test	A2	Entry 2

PET is taken by more than 80,000 people each year in more than 80 countries, and is a valuable qualification if you want to work or study abroad or to develop a career in international business. It is also useful preparation for higher level exams, such as FCE (First Certificate in English), CAE (Certificate in Advanced English) and CPE (Certificate of Proficiency in English).

If you can deal with everyday written and spoken communications (e.g. read simple textbooks and articles, write simple personal letters, make notes during a meeting), then this is the exam for you.

Topics

These are the topics used in the PET exam:

Clothes
Daily life
Education
Entertainment and media
Environment
Food and drink
Free time
Health, medicine and
   exercise

Hobbies and leisure
House and home
Language
Natural world
People
Personal feelings, opinions
   and experiences
Personal identification
Places and buildings

Relations with other people
Services
Shopping
Social interaction
Sport
Transport
Travel and holidays
Weather
Work and jobs

PET content: an overview

Paper	Name	Timing	Content	Test focus
Paper 1	Reading/ Writing	1 hour 30 minutes	Reading: Five parts which test a range of reading skills with a variety of texts, ranging from very short notices to longer continuous texts. Writing: Three parts which test a range of writing skills.	Assessment of candidates' ability to understand the meaning of written English at word, phrase, sentence, paragraph and whole text level. Assessment of candidates' ability to produce straightforward written English, ranging from producing variations on simple sentences to pieces of continuous text.
Paper 2	Listening	35 minutes (approx.)	Four parts ranging from short exchanges to longer dialogues and monologues.	Assessment of candidates' ability to understand dialogues and monologues in both informal and neutral settings on a range of everyday topics.
Paper 3	Speaking	10–12 minutes per pair of candidates	Four parts: In Part 1, candidates interact with an examiner; In Parts 2 and 4 they interact with another candidate; In Part 3, they have an extended individual long turn.	Assessment of candidates' ability to express themselves in order to carry out functions at *Threshold* level. To ask and to understand questions and make appropriate responses. To talk freely on matters of personal interest.

Paper 1: Reading and Writing

Paper format
The Reading component contains five parts. The Writing component contains three parts.

Number of questions
Reading has 35 questions; Writing has seven questions.

Sources
Authentic and adapted-authentic real world notices; newspapers and magazines; simplified encyclopaedias; brochures and leaflets; websites.

Answering
Candidates indicate answers by shading lozenges (Reading), or writing answers (Writing) on an answer sheet.

Timing
1 hour 30 minutes.

Marks
Reading: Each of the 35 questions carries one mark. This is weighted so that this comprises 25% of total marks for the whole examination.

Writing: Questions 1–5 carry one mark each. Question 6 is marked out of five; and Question 7/8 is marked out of 15. This gives a total of 25 which represents 25% of total marks for the whole examination.

Preparing for the Reading component

To prepare for the Reading component, you should read a variety of authentic texts, for example, newspapers and magazines, non-fiction books, and other sources of factual material, such as leaflets, brochures and websites. It is also a good idea to practise reading (and writing) short communicative messages, including notes, cards and emails. Remember you won't always need to understand every word in order to be able to do a task in the exam.

Before the examination, think about the time you need to do each part. It is usually approximately 50 minutes on the Reading component and 40 minutes on the Writing component.

Reading			
Part	**Task Type and Format**	**Task Focus**	**Number of questions**
1	Three-option multiple choice. Five short discrete texts: signs and messages, postcards, notes, emails, labels etc., plus one example.	Reading real-world notices and other short texts for the main message.	5
2	Matching. Five items in the form of descriptions of people to match to eight short adapted-authentic texts.	Reading multiple texts for specific information and detailed comprehension.	5
3	True/False. Ten items with an adapted-authentic long text.	Processing a factual text. Scanning for specific information while disregarding redundant material.	10
4	Four-option multiple choice. Five items with an adapted-authentic long text.	Reading for detailed comprehension: understanding attitude, opinion and writer purpose. Reading for gist, inference and global meaning.	5
5	Four-option multiple-choice cloze. Ten items, plus an integrated example, with an adapted-authentic text drawn from a variety of sources. The text is of a factual or narrative nature.	Understanding of vocabulary and grammar in a short text, and understanding the lexico-structural patterns in the text.	10

Preparing for the Writing component

Part 1

You have to complete five sentences which will test your grammar. There is an example, showing exactly what the task involves. You should write between one and three words to fill this gap. The second sentence, when complete, must mean the same as the first sentence.

It is essential to spell correctly and no marks will be given if a word is misspelled. You will also lose the mark if you produce an answer of more than three words, even if your writing includes the correct answer.

Part 2

You have to produce a short communicative message of between 35 and 45 words in length. You are told who you are writing to and why, and you must include three content points. These are clearly laid out with bullet points in the question. To gain top marks, all three points must be in your answer, so it is important to read the question carefully and plan what you will include. Marks will not be deducted for small errors.

Before the exam, you need to practise writing answers of the correct length. Answers that are too short or too long will probably lose marks.

The General Mark Scheme below is used with a Task-specific Mark Scheme (see pages 104, 117, 129 and 141).

General Mark Scheme for Writing Part 2

Mark	Criteria
5	All content elements covered appropriately. Message clearly communicated to reader.
4	All content elements adequately dealt with. Message communicated successfully, on the whole.
3	All content elements attempted. Message requires some effort by the reader. or One content element omitted but others clearly communicated.
2	Two content elements omitted, or unsuccessfully dealt with. Message only partly communicated to reader. or Script may be slightly short (20–25 words).
1	Little relevant content and/or message requires excessive effort by the reader, or short (10–19 words).
0	Totally irrelevant or totally incomprehensible or too short (under 10 words).

Part 3

You have a choice of task: either a story or an informal letter. You need to write about 100 words for both tasks. Answers below 80 words will receive fewer marks. Answers longer than 100 words may receive fewer marks.

Make sure you practise enough before the exam. Reading simplified readers in English will give you ideas for story writing. Also writing to a penfriend or e-pal will give you useful practice.

Mark Scheme for Writing Part 3

Band 5 – the candidate's writing fully achieves the desired effect on the target reader. The use of language will be confident and ambitious for the level, including a wide range of structures and vocabulary within the task set. Coherence, within the constraints of the level, will be achieved by the use of simple linking devices, and the response will be well organised. Errors which do occur will be minor and non-impeding, perhaps due to ambitious attempts at more complex language. Overall, no effort will be required of the reader.

Band 4 – the candidate's writing will achieve the desired effect on the target reader. The use of language will be fairly ambitious for the level, including a range of structures and vocabulary within the task set. There will be some linking of sentences and evidence of organisation. Some errors will occur, although these will be generally non-impeding. Overall, only a little effort will be required of the reader.

Band 3 – the candidate's writing may struggle at times to achieve the desired effect on the target reader. The use of language, including the range of structure and vocabulary, will be unambitious, or, if ambitious, it will be flawed. There will be some attempt at organisation but the linking of sentences will not always be maintained. A number of errors may be present, although these will be mostly non-impeding. Overall, some effort will be required of the reader.

Band 2 – the candidate's writing struggles to achieve the desired effect on the target reader. The use of language, including the range of structure and vocabulary, will tend to be simplistic, limited, or repetitive. The response may be incoherent, and include erratic use of punctuation. There will be numerous errors which will sometimes impede communication. Overall, considerable effort will be required of the reader.

Band 1 – the candidate's writing has a negative effect on the target reader. The use of language will be severely restricted, and there will be no evidence of a range of structures and vocabulary. The response will be seriously incoherent, and may include an absence of punctuation. Language will be very poorly controlled and the response will be difficult to understand. Overall, excessive effort will be required of the reader.

Band 0 – there may be too little language for assessment, or the response may be totally illegible; the content may be impossible to understand, or completely irrelevant to the task.

Writing			
Part	**Task Type and Format**	**Task Focus**	**Number of questions**
1	Sentence transformations. Five items, plus an integrated example, that are theme-related. Candidates are given sentences and then asked to complete similar sentences using a different structural pattern so that the sentence still has the same meaning.	Control and understanding of Threshold/PET grammatical structures. Rephrasing and reformulating information.	5
2	Short communicative message. Candidates are prompted to write a short message in the form of a postcard, note, email, etc. The prompt takes the form of a rubric to respond to.	A short piece of writing of 35–45 words focusing on communication of specific messages.	1
3	A longer piece of continuous writing. There is a choice of two questions, an informal letter or a story. Candidates are primarily assessed on their ability to use and control a range of Threshold-level language. Coherent organisation, spelling and punctuation are also assessed.	Writing about 100 words focusing on control and range of language.	1

Paper 2: Listening

Paper format
This paper contains four parts.

Number of questions
25

Text types
All texts are based on authentic situations.

Answering
Candidates indicate answers either by shading lozenges (Parts 1, 2 and 4) or writing answers (Part 3) on an answer sheet. Candidates record their answers on the question paper as they listen. They are then given six minutes at the end of the test to copy these on to the answer sheet.

Recording information
Each text is heard twice. Recordings will contain a variety of accents corresponding to standard variants of native speaker accents.

Timing
About 35 minutes, plus six minutes to transfer answers.

Marks
Each question carries one mark. This gives a total of 25 marks, which represents 25% of total marks for the whole examination.

Part	Task Type and Format	Task Focus	Number of questions
1	Multiple choice (discrete). Short neutral or informal monologues or dialogues. Seven discrete three-option multiple-choice items with visuals, plus one example.	Listening to identify key information from short exchanges.	7
2	Multiple choice. Longer monologue or interview (with one main speaker). Six three-option multiple-choice items.	Listening to identify specific information and detailed meaning.	6
3	Gap-fill. Longer monologue. Six gaps to fill in. Candidates need to write one or more words in each space.	Listening to identify, understand and interpret information.	6
4	True/False. Longer informal dialogue. Candidates need to decide whether six statements are correct or incorrect.	Listening for detailed meaning, and to identify the attitudes and opinions of the speakers.	6

Preparing for the Listening paper

You will hear the instructions for each task on the recording, and see them on the exam paper.
In Part 1, there is also an example text and task to show you how to record your answers.
In Parts 2, 3 and 4, the instructions are followed by a pause; you should read the questions in that part then. This will help you prepare for the listening.

The best preparation for the listening paper is to listen to authentic spoken English at this level. Having discussions provides a good authentic source of listening practice, as does listening to the teacher. You can also listen to texts to give you practice in understanding different voices and styles of delivery.

Paper 3: Speaking

Paper format

The standard format is two candidates and two examiners. One of the examiners acts as an interlocutor and the other as an assessor. The interlocutor directs the test, while the assessor takes no part in the interaction.

Timing

10–12 minutes per pair of candidates.

Marks

Candidates are assessed on their performance throughout the test. There are a total of 25 marks in Paper 3, making 25% of the total score for the whole examination.

Part	Task Type and Format	Task Focus	Timing
1	Each candidate interacts with the interlocutor. The interlocutor asks the candidates questions in turn, using standardised questions.	Giving information of a factual, personal kind. The candidates respond to questions about present circumstances, past experiences and future plans.	2–3 minutes
2	Simulated situation. Candidates interact with each other. Visual stimulus is given to the candidates to aid the discussion task. The interlocutor sets up the activity using a standardised rubric.	Using functional language to make and respond to suggestions, discuss alternatives, make recommendations and negotiate agreement.	2–3 minutes
3	Extended turn. A colour photograph is given to each candidate in turn and they are asked to talk about it for up to a minute. Both photographs relate to the same topic.	Describing photographs and managing discourse, using appropriate vocabulary, in a longer turn.	3 minutes
4	General conversation. Candidates interact with each other. The topic of the conversation develops the theme established in Part 3. The interlocutor sets up the activity using a standardised rubric.	The candidates talk together about their opinions, likes/dislikes, preferences, experiences, habits, etc.	3 minutes

Assessment

Throughout the test, you are assessed on your language skills, not your personality, intelligence or knowledge of the world. You must, however, be prepared to develop the conversation, where appropriate, and respond to the tasks set. Prepared speeches are not acceptable.

You are assessed on your own individual performance and not in relation to each other. Both examiners assess you. The interlocutor awards a mark for global achievement; the assessor awards marks according to: Grammar and Vocabulary, Discourse Management, Pronunciation and Interactive Communication.

Grammar and Vocabulary
This refers to the accurate and appropriate use of grammatical forms and vocabulary. It also includes the range of both grammatical forms and vocabulary. Performance is viewed in terms of the overall effectiveness of the language used in dealing with the tasks.

Discourse Management
This refers to the coherence, extent and relevance of each individual's contribution. On this scale, the ability to maintain a coherent flow of language is assessed, either within a single utterance or over a string of utterances. Also assessed here is how relevant the contributions are to what has gone before.

Pronunciation
This refers to the candidate's ability to produce comprehensible utterances to fulfil the task requirements. This includes stress, rhythm and intonation, as well as individual sounds. Examiners put themselves in the position of the non-language specialist and assess the overall impact of the pronunciation and the degree of effort required to understand the candidate. Different varieties of English e.g. British, North American, Australian, etc., are acceptable, provided they are used consistently throughout the test.

Interactive Communication
This scale refers to the candidate's ability to use language to achieve meaningful communication. This includes initiating and responding without undue hesitation, the ability to use interactive strategies to maintain or repair communication, and sensitivity to the norms of turn-taking.

Further information

More information about PET or any other Cambridge ESOL examination can be obtained from Cambridge ESOL at the address below or from the website at www.CambridgeESOL.org

University of Cambridge ESOL Examinations
1 Hills Road
Cambridge CB1 2EU
United Kingdom

Telephone +44 1223 553355
Fax: +44 1223 460278
e-mail: ESOLHelpdesk@Cambridgeassessment.org.uk

Test 1

PAPER 1 READING AND WRITING TEST (1 hour 30 minutes)

READING

Part 1

Questions 1–5

Look at the text in each question.
What does it say?
Mark the correct letter **A**, **B** or **C** on your answer sheet.

Example:

0

A Valuable objects are removed at night.

B Valuables should not be left in the van.

C This van is locked at night.

Answer:

1

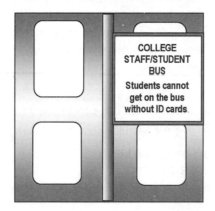

A This bus service cannot be used by college staff unless they show ID cards.

B Students can get their ID cards on the bus.

C Students are not allowed on the bus unless they have ID cards.

2

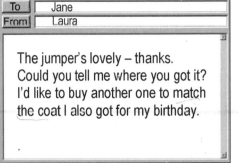

To   Jane
From   Laura

The jumper's lovely – thanks.
Could you tell me where you got it?
I'd like to buy another one to match
the coat I also got for my birthday.

A Laura liked the jumper Jane bought, but needs it in a different size.

B Laura wants to try to get the same jumper in a different colour.

C Laura received two jumpers which were the same, so wants to exchange one.

3

UNIVERSITY HOLIDAYS

From next Friday, the library will be closed during weekends and evenings.

The library will

A have shorter opening hours until next Friday.

B change its opening hours next Friday.

C open again to students next Friday.

4

Mark,
We went on a bus sightseeing tour of the city yesterday. We didn't stop anywhere but saw more than you would on foot.

Jo

A Jo is pleased with the number of things she saw from the bus.

B Jo regrets not having walked around the city to look at the sights.

C Jo thinks there are better sightseeing tours than the one she took.

5

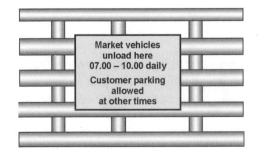

Market vehicles
unload here
07.00 – 10.00 daily

Customer parking
allowed
at other times

A Customers may park outside the market for up to three hours.

B You may unload your vehicle here at any time.

C Customers may park here at times when vehicles are not unloading.

Part 2

Questions 6–10

The people below all want to visit a museum.
On the opposite page there are descriptions of eight museums.
Decide which museum would be the most suitable for the following people.
For questions **6–10**, mark the correct letter (**A–H**) on your answer sheet.

6

Cristina wants to visit a museum with her daughter to see how people used to live. They want to have lunch there and buy some presents to take home. They will go by car.

7

Joanne wants to visit a museum and see people making things. She has no car and would like to have lunch there.

8

Carl's hobby is painting pictures, so he would like to see the work of other painters who live in the area. He wants to have a snack at the museum. He travels by public transport.

9

Duncan wants to find out where local people worked in the past and what they did in their spare time. He wants to buy a book about the exhibition. He travels by bus.

10

The Cannavaro family want to walk around a site which offers opportunities for the whole family to take part in activities. They want somewhere pleasant to eat their own sandwiches. They have a car.

MUSEUMS IN THE AREA

A **Stackworth Museum** tells the history of the famous Stackworth family, and gives information about other well-known local people. These include poets, artists and writers. There is an excellent café and a car park.

B **Charberth Museum** is near the main bus station and has a rich collection of objects, 19th-century paintings and photographs showing life in the town over the centuries – the jobs people did and how they entertained themselves. An accompanying book showing the works on display is available from the Museum Shop as well as some attractive gifts. There is no café.

C **Fairley Museum** is arranged like an old-fashioned village. You can see people working at their trades to produce tools, pots and even boats using traditional skills. There is a small picnic area in the car park but most people eat in the excellent café. The museum is on a bus route.

D **Westerleigh Museum** is near the bus station, and contains exhibitions showing the town's development. In a separate room there are works by some well-known artists as well as changing exhibitions of work by local artists. Sandwiches, cakes and hot drinks are on sale in the café.

E The rooms in **Scotwood Manor** are furnished as they were 100 years ago. The staff spend the day as people did then and are happy to explain what it was like. There are activity sheets for children and a shop with books, souvenirs and cards, as well as a good café and car park.

F Freshwater was once an important fishing port. **Freshwater Museum**, inside the old harbour office, shows how the town developed and later became a tourist centre. There is an activity room for young children with DVDs, a large picnic area, car park, and good bus service.

G Set in beautiful countryside, the **Woodlands Museum** is arranged like a village of 100 years ago. To learn more about this period, visitors are encouraged to spend time doing practical things such as making pots and cooking. There is an adventure playground with a picnic area under the trees and parking.

H **Middleworth Museum** is full of objects from the past, which tell the story of different people who worked in the area, from factory workers to the men who built the canal and the railway. There is a Family Folder of things to do. The museum has a café and is near the bus and railway station.

Part 3

Questions 11–20

Look at the sentences below about The Short Story Society.
Read the text on the opposite page to decide if each sentence is correct or incorrect.
If it is correct, mark **A** on your answer sheet.
If it is not correct, mark **B** on your answer sheet.

___

11   The Short Story Society has existed for over a century.

12   *Short Story Review* publishes work by inexperienced writers.

13   Articles from one of the Society's magazines are available on the internet.

14   Writers entering the National Short Story Competition must choose a subject suggested by the Society.

15   It costs £5 for members of the Society to enter the National Short Story Competition.

16   Each year, ten winning writers will be offered contracts to publish their own books.

17   The Short Story Society visits schools to give pupils help with writing.

18   Society members can attend regular events at the Writers' Café.

19   The Writers' Café is situated just outside London.

20   Children from anywhere in the world are able to become members of the Society.

www.shortstorysoc.com

Membership

email enquiries:membership@shortstorysoc.com

The Short Story Society exists to help writers in Britain today. Started in 1899, the Short Story Society is now one of Britain's most active arts organisations.

- **Society Magazines**
- **National Short Story Competition**
- **Education**
- **The Writers' Café**
- **Becoming a Member**

Society Magazines

We produce a range of excellent magazines, including the popular *Short Story Review*. This magazine includes short stories by some of Britain's top writers, as well as providing plenty of opportunities for new writers to have their work printed. Another magazine, *Short Story News*, has interviews with writers and is packed with information about events, competitions, festivals and the writing scene in general. To see a selection of articles from recent issues, follow the links on this website.

National Short Story Competition

We run the National Short Story Competition, the biggest competition of its kind. It is open to anyone aged 18 and over and short stories on any topic are accepted. Short stories should be between 1,000 and 1,500 words long. There is no entry fee for anyone belonging to the Society (non-members pay an entry fee of £5). The competition runs from April until the end of October each year. The ten best entries will appear in the Society's annual book of short stories. The actual winner will receive a publishing contract to produce his or her own collection of short stories.

Education

For nearly thirty years the Society has taken writers into classrooms, providing children and teachers with new ideas and building confidence in their own writing. Current projects include the *Young Writer of the Year*, which was started in 1998 and is open to writers aged 11–18. All winners receive book prizes and are invited to study on a five-day course taught by professional writers.

The Writers' Café

The Writers' Café is the social centre of the Society. Relaxed and stylish, with freshly cooked vegetarian food, excellent coffees and cold drinks, it is the ideal place to look through the Society's magazines. The Café also provides monthly exhibitions, short courses and readings. Its location is in the heart of London, and it is open from 11.00 am to 10.00 pm Monday to Friday and 11.00 am to 8.00 pm on Saturday. Society members receive discounts on selected products and events.

Becoming a Member

We have members worldwide, and anyone aged eighteen or over is welcome to join. If you are interested in joining The Short Story Society, click here and fill out a registration form.

Return to **Top**   Go to **Short Story News**

Part 4

Questions 21–25

Read the text and questions below.
For each question, mark the correct letter **A**, **B**, **C** or **D** on your answer sheet.

New TV Star
Caroline Benson talks about her first TV role

'I never expected to spend some of my first year at university filming *The Finnegans*. I'd only ever acted at school, but I'd loved the book since I was eleven. My grandmother used to say I was just like Polly Finnegan and I always imagined myself playing her.

I'd taken a year off to go travelling before university. While I was in Chile, my mother emailed me to say there were plans to turn the book into a TV drama. I knew I had to go for the part. She was surprised at first, but sent my photograph to the director and persuaded him to meet me. I flew back and got the part.

The outdoor filming started a week into term, so I got permission from the university to be away for three weeks. Once I was back at university, I got up at 6.00 am to write the essays I'd missed. I didn't tell my university friends, but they found out and thought it was great.

It was an amazing experience – I'm so lucky. After university, I definitely want to make acting my career. I'm not from an acting family, though my grandfather was an opera singer. I've tried for other TV parts but haven't received any offers yet.

I don't know how I managed it all, because I had a full social life too. When filming finished, I hardly knew what to do. I've since appeared in two college plays. Unfortunately, I haven't been home much and now my first year at university is over, I'm off to Greece for the summer with friends.'

21   In this text, Caroline Benson is

    A   advising students to finish studying before taking up acting.
    B   describing how pleased she was about this opportunity to act.
    C   warning other young people that acting is a difficult career.
    D   explaining why she has always wanted to be an actor.

22   Why did Caroline decide to try for a part in *The Finnegans*?

    A   She thought the book would make a great TV drama.
    B   She agreed with her grandmother that she should apply.
    C   She felt she was perfect for the part of Polly.
    D   She was anxious about starting university.

23 What does Caroline say about her mother?

    A   She encouraged Caroline to keep travelling.
    B   She felt Caroline would be a good actor.
    C   She was sorry she had emailed Caroline.
    D   She helped Caroline to get the part.

24 How did Caroline manage to find time to do the filming?

    A   She missed lectures and hoped nobody would notice.
    B   She delayed going to university until filming was over.
    C   She took time off and did her college work later.
    D   She asked her friends to help with her essays.

25 Which of the following would Caroline write to a penfriend?

A	B
I'm going to continue with my studies, but hope to have the opportunity to do another TV programme soon.	Now I've finished both the filming and my first year at university, I plan to spend more time with my family.

C	D
I enjoyed filming the TV drama but I've missed having a social life – I don't know what to do at weekends.	Acting is more difficult than I'd expected, but I've learned a lot from other members of my family who work in the business.

Part 5

Questions 26–35

Read the text below and choose the correct word for each space.
For each question, mark the correct letter **A**, **B**, **C** or **D** on your answer sheet.

Example:

0	**A** most	**B** more	**C** very	**D** too

Answer:

0	A B C D

Grass

Grass is probably the **(0)** .... successful living plant in the world. There are over 9,000 different types of grasses and they are **(26)** .... in every region on the earth. They are the **(27)** .... flowering plants that can exist in the freezing **(28)** .... of the Arctic and the Antarctic.

Grasslands support a wide range of animal life, from tiny insects and birds to huge animals like cows and lions. All of them **(29)** .... on grass in one way or another.

Grass **(30)** .... very quickly after it is cut or **(31)** .... Unlike other plants, the new leaves grow from **(32)** .... the soil, not from the top of the plant. That is **(33)** .... large families of animals are able to live together in one area. As **(34)** .... as they have eaten all the grass there, a fresh meal is always **(35)** .... because the plants start to grow again.

26	**A** noticed	**B** realised	**C** caught	**D** found
27	**A** single	**B** one	**C** only	**D** special
28	**A** environment	**B** scene	**C** situation	**D** background
29	**A** depend	**B** build	**C** turn	**D** hang
30	**A** repeats	**B** recovers	**C** reduces	**D** remains
31	**A** hurt	**B** broken	**C** injured	**D** damaged
32	**A** beside	**B** behind	**C** below	**D** beyond
33	**A** why	**B** where	**C** what	**D** when
34	**A** fast	**B** soon	**C** quickly	**D** often
35	**A** available	**B** present	**C** free	**D** complete

WRITING

Part 1

Questions 1–5

Here are some sentences about a sports centre.
For each question, complete the second sentence so that it means the same as the first.
Use no more than three words.
Write only the missing words on your answer sheet.
You may use this page for any rough work.

Example:

0 Sarah started working at the sports centre two months ago.

Sarah has worked at the sports centre .... **two months.**

Answer: | **0** | *for* |

---

1 Sarah asked me if I was still a member of the sports centre.

Sarah asked me, '... **still a member of the sports centre?'**

2 Non-members cannot enter the sports centre without a ticket.

Non-members aren't .... **to enter the sports centre without a ticket.**

3 Trainers must be worn in the sports centre at all times.

You must .... **trainers in the sports centre at all times.**

4 Football is the most popular sport at the centre.

Football is .... **than any other sport at the sports centre.**

5 Sarah thinks the sports centre is too small for the town.

Sarah thinks the sports centre is not .... **for the town.**

Part 2

Question 6

You want to borrow your English friend Sam's bicycle.

Write an email to your English friend Sam. In your email, you should

- explain why you need to borrow the bicycle
- say how long you will need it for
- tell Sam when you will return it.

Write **35–45 words** on your answer sheet.

Part 3

Write an answer to **one** of the questions (**7** or **8**) in this part.
Write your answer in about **100 words** on your answer sheet.
Mark the question number in the box at the top of your answer sheet.

Question 7

- This is part of a letter you receive from an English friend.

> A new restaurant has just opened in my town and it's
> wonderful. Have you got a favourite restaurant?
> Tell me about the food and what you like about the
> restaurant.

- Now write a letter to your friend about a restaurant.
- Write your **letter** on your answer sheet.

Question 8

- Your English teacher wants you to write a story.
- Your story must begin with this sentence:

I was on the beach when my mobile phone rang.

- Write your **story** on your answer sheet.

PAPER 2   LISTENING TEST   approx 35 minutes
(including 6 minutes transfer time)

Part 1

Questions 1–7

There are seven questions in this part.
For each question there are three pictures and a short recording.
Choose the correct picture and put a tick (✓) in the box below it.

Example: Where is the girl's hat?

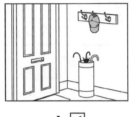  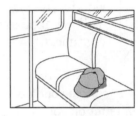

A ✓   B ☐   C ☐

---

1   What was damaged in the storm?

 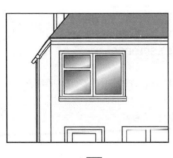 

A ☐   B ☐   C ☐

2   What present does the man decide to take?

 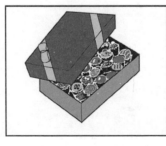 

A ☐   B ☐   C ☐

3   Which is the woman's jacket?

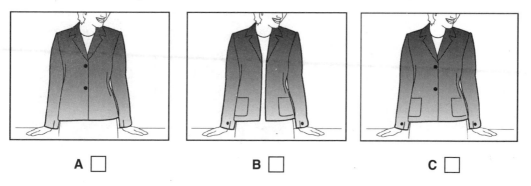

A ☐   B ☐   C ☐

4   Which sport is <u>not</u> included in the price of the holiday?

A ☐   B ☐   C ☐

5   Which postcard will they send?

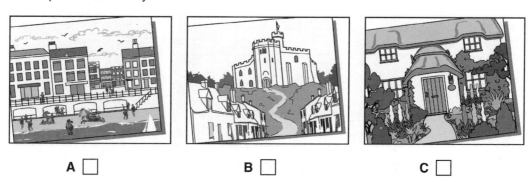

A ☐   B ☐   C ☐

6   Where do they decide to go?

A ☐   B ☐   C ☐

7   What will the boy do first?

A ☐   B ☐   C ☐

Part 2

Questions 8–13

You will hear an English woman called Britta talking to an interviewer about her life in Berlin, the capital of Germany.

For each question, put a tick (✓) in the correct box.

---

8 How long has Britta lived in Berlin?

    A ☐ four years

    B ☐ six years

    C ☐ twenty years

9 What does Britta say about living in Berlin?

    A ☐ She can't sleep at night because of the traffic noise.

    B ☐ She misses the museums and theatres in Bonn.

    C ☐ She likes living in a big, busy city.

10 The area of Berlin where Britta lives is

    A ☐ a rather expensive place to live.

    B ☐ a good place to eat out.

    C ☐ a long way from the city centre.

11 How does Britta usually travel around in Berlin?

    A ☐ She walks.

    B ☐ She uses her bicycle.

    C ☐ She uses the tram or bus.

12 Britta says that her nephew, Philippe, likes going

A ☐ to the park with her.

B ☐ to the shops with his parents.

C ☐ to a gallery with her.

13 Britta has lots of friends who

A ☐ live near her.

B ☐ work with her.

C ☐ are still in England.

Part 3

Questions 14–19

You will hear a man called Stephen Mills talking to a group of people about a trip to India to see tigers.
For each question, fill in the missing information in the numbered space.

THE TIGER TOUR

Stephen's profession: **(14)** ....

Date of departure: **(15)** ....

Number of tourists in group: **(16)** ....

Type of accommodation: **(17)** ....

Means of transport in the park: – open truck in the north

– **(18)** .... in the south

Meal <u>not</u> included: **(19)** .... on the last day

Part 4

Questions 20–25

Look at the six sentences for this part.
You will hear a conversation between a boy, Carl, and a girl, Susanna, about a school concert.
Decide if each sentence is correct or incorrect.
If it is correct, put a tick (✓) in the box under **A** for **YES**. If it is not correct, put a tick (✓) in the box under **B** for **NO**.

		A YES	B NO
20	Susanna feels shy about playing her violin in public.	☐	☐
21	Carl and Susanna share the same opinion about practising their instruments regularly.	☐	☐
22	Susanna's parents refuse to allow her to give up violin lessons.	☐	☐
23	Carl's aim is to have a career in music.	☐	☐
24	Susanna thinks she would enjoy working in another country.	☐	☐
25	Carl persuades Susanna to take part in the concert.	☐	☐

About the Speaking test

The Speaking test lasts about 10 to 12 minutes. You take the test with another candidate. There are two examiners in the room. One examiner talks to you and the other examiner listens to you. Both the examiners give you marks.

Part 1

The examiners introduce themselves and then one examiner asks you and your partner to say your names and spell them. This examiner then asks you questions about yourself, your daily life, interests, etc.

Part 2

The examiner asks you to talk about something together and gives you a drawing to help you.

Part 3

You each have a chance to talk by yourselves. The examiner gives you a colour photograph to look at and asks you to talk about it. When you have finished talking, the examiner gives your partner a different photograph to look at and to talk about.

Part 4

The examiner asks you and your partner to say more about the subject of the photographs in Part 3. You may be asked to give your opinion or to talk about something that has happened to you.

Test 2

PAPER 1 READING AND WRITING TEST (1 hour 30 minutes)

Part 1

Questions 1–5

Look at the text in each question.
What does it say?
Mark the correct letter **A**, **B** or **C** on your answer sheet.

Example:

0

A Buy three films for the price of two.

B Get a free film with every one you buy.

C Films bought here are printed free.

Answer:

1

Jennie,
    The garage rang – your new tyres have arrived. They can't fit them until next week. Please let them know today which day will be convenient.

Jennie has to

A ask another garage to fit her tyres.

B arrange a time for the garage to fit the new tyres.

C collect the new tyres from the garage.

2

Would anyone who knows anything about the damaged window in the school library please report to my office before the end of the day.
Mrs Swan

What does Mrs Swan want to do today?

A repair damage done to the library

B discover how a window got broken

C find out who uses the library

3

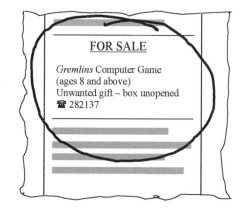

FOR SALE

Gremlins Computer Game
(ages 8 and above)
Unwanted gift – box unopened
☎ 282137

A The owner of the computer game that is for sale has never used it.

B The computer game is for sale because the owner is too old for it.

C The person selling the computer game no longer wants to play with it.

4

Students have free internet access until midday on weekdays and all day at weekends.

A There is a charge for internet access at weekends.

B Students must always pay to use the internet in the afternoons.

C It doesn't cost anything to use the internet on weekday mornings.

5

Guess who I met on this mountain! My tennis hero! I was breathless because of the climb, so unfortunately couldn't speak to ask him for a photo of us together.
Amanda

Amanda regrets that she

A didn't recognise her tennis hero from his photo.

B couldn't climb high enough to photograph her tennis hero.

C didn't have her photograph taken with her tennis hero.

Part 2

Questions 6–10

The people below are all visiting the same city in Britain and want to find a suitable hotel.
On the opposite page there are descriptions of eight hotels.
Decide which hotel would be the most suitable for the following people.
For questions **6–10**, mark the correct letter (**A–H**) on your answer sheet.

6

Stephen is looking for a top-quality hotel which is convenient for the airport, to hold a meeting with visiting German publishers. They will stay overnight and want to take some exercise outdoors after the meeting.

7

Karl and Monika want to stay in the city centre overnight at a hotel offering good local food. The next morning they plan to see the main sights. They are not worried about the cost of the hotel.

8

James and Denise want a modern, medium-priced hotel in the city, but will eat out during their stay. They also want to see some films in the evenings, somewhere near their hotel.

9

David and Katrina have just started work after leaving college and haven't got much money, so they want a reasonably priced hotel. They like country walks and watersports.

10

Sue and Belinda want to stay somewhere in the city centre that offers a variety of evening entertainment within the hotel, including live music.

HOTELS

A The **Salisbury Hotel** is a top hotel with a health club, swimming pool, shops and a fully-equipped business centre. Within the hotel are three international restaurants, one with a French chef. The hotel is conveniently located close to the motorway, though airport users should allow plenty of time because traffic is usually heavy.

B The **Cumberland Hotel** is well placed for sightseeing on a busy city street, in a district which is full of interesting shops. Rooms are expensive but comfortable and the hotel serves excellent food, typical of the area. A piano player entertains guests every night in the bar.

C The **Rathmore Hotel** offers good value accommodation, with wonderful English food in the restaurant. The hotel is well-known for its small orchestra which plays while guests have dinner. It is on the eastern edge of the city but special sightseeing buses are available to take guests into the centre (the trip takes over an hour in traffic).

D The **Russell Hotel** is close to the airport, and has quiet, comfortable rooms. However, the journey to the city centre can take time, and prices are above average. Delicious local food is served in the restaurant, and its conference rooms and business facilities are excellent. The hotel is surrounded by woodland, offers a golf course, and there are pleasant walks around the nearby lake.

E The newly-built **Aviemore Hotel** is small but in the centre of the city's cinema, restaurant and nightclub district. Rooms are clean, comfortable and reasonably priced, although the food is rather basic. There is an electronic games arcade in the hotel.

F The **Padnal** is an older hotel in the heart of the city, with ground-floor rooms opening onto a country-style garden. Prices are reasonable. There is a sports centre and a small cinema and nightclub. A band performs every evening in the hotel restaurant, where excellent French food is served. Airport buses pick up from the hotel.

G The **Westmore Hotel** is in beautiful countryside to the east of the city. It is peaceful and inexpensive, although the accommodation is basic. There are opportunities nearby for sailing and diving, and a lot of interesting routes to explore on foot.

H Although the prices at the **Grange Hotel** are higher than at many city-centre hotels, it has a lot to offer. It shares a modern complex with nightclubs, cinemas, shops and conference facilities, 20 kilometres west of the centre. Trains run from the nearby railway station to the city centre and the airport, although journeys can take up to an hour.

Part 3

Questions 11–20

Look at the sentences below about tourist flights over the continent of Antarctica.
Read the text on the opposite page to decide if each sentence is correct or incorrect.
If it is correct, mark **A** on your answer sheet.
If it is not correct, mark **B** on your answer sheet.

11   Sightseeing flights to Antarctica are available for a limited period each year.

12   You may have to book a flight without being certain when it will happen.

13   Passengers have views of Antarctic scenery for more than half their flight.

14   Passengers can speak to people who have experience of working in Antarctica.

15   Special video equipment operates during the whole flight.

16   People are asked to stay sitting down so that everybody can see better.

17   There is an advantage in sitting on one particular side of the plane.

18   Before departure, the pilot chooses between a number of possible routes.

19   A special attraction of the trip is having clear views of Antarctic wildlife.

20   Passengers have the chance to put on clothes designed for travel in Antarctica.

ANTARCTICA SIGHTSEEING FLIGHTS WEBSITE

Next flight 31 December!

Welcome to the website. Here is all you need to know before booking a flight.

During the brief Antarctic summer, Antarctica Sightseeing Flights takes tourists in a full-size passenger plane (Boeing 747) from Sydney, Australia, over the continent of Antarctica and back.

Flight dates for next year are not definite yet, but if you make a booking now, your deposit is transferable if we need to change the day.

Questions
These are answers to the most frequently asked questions about Antarctica Sightseeing Flights.

How long is the flight?
The average flight is 12 hours. About four hours into the flight, we usually see the first sea ice and icebergs. We spend four hours over Antarctica and the remaining time travelling home. On the way to and from the continent, Antarctica experts who have lived on scientific research stations there give talks on the environment and history, and answer questions. A camera next to the pilot, which is linked to the video system on board, gives you a pilot's eye view throughout, from take-off to landing.

Will I get a seat next to a window?
All passengers are given two boarding passes. At the halfway point of the flight, passengers are asked to move to the seat shown on their second boarding pass. Business and first class passengers will have a window seat for half of the flight and a next-to-window seat for the other half. Economy passengers will have a window seat or the seat next to a window seat for half of the flight and an end of row seat for the other half of the flight. While over Antarctica, we encourage passengers to get up from their seats and move about the plane, allowing everyone to share the sightseeing opportunities. The pilot flies in long 'figure 8s' over various points of interest to allow these amazing sights to be seen equally well from both sides of the plane.

What happens if the weather is bad?
We have 17 different approved flight plans. Our captain looks at the satellite cloud picture on the morning of the flight and selects the direction which promises the clearest views.

Will I see penguins and other wildlife?
As most Antarctic wildlife lives at sea level, over 3,000 metres below the plane, we can't see them in any detail. We do not land on Antarctica, primarily for environmental reasons. To experience Antarctic wildlife, you would need to join a boat tour.

Can I take photographs?
Definitely! All cameras are welcome. We even provide a few fun onboard photo opportunities where you can experience what it is like to wear Antarctic cold weather clothes.

GALLERY >

FLIGHT FACTS >

FLIGHT DATES >

PRICES >

BOOK NOW >

Part 4

Questions 21–25

Read the text and questions below.
For each question, mark the correct letter **A**, **B**, **C** or **D** on your answer sheet.

Maria Mutola
Former 800 metres Olympic champion

In 1988, Maria Mutola was playing football as the only girl in an all-boys team in a local competition in Mozambique. 'We won,' she said. 'At first no one thought it was a problem that I was a girl. But then the team we beat complained.'

The story appeared in a local newspaper and José Craveirinha, who had encouraged other African athletes, learnt about Maria. He went to meet her and found her kicking a ball around outside the football club. He realised immediately that she was fast. 'He talked to me about athletics. I had no idea what he meant. The only sport I knew about was football. Then he bought me running shoes and took me training. It was such hard work and my legs really ached.' But José visited her parents and persuaded them she could be successful and this would help end their poverty. They agreed to let him take her away to train.

In 1991, she finally accepted an invitation to train in the United States. She had refused previously because she knew she would miss her family. Her background was unlike those of the girls she met in the US. She explains, 'They were good athletes but, while I worried about my parents having enough to eat, they worried about dresses and make-up. They knew very little about me and even less about my problems. But I knew I was lucky to be there. The trainers were brilliant and I learnt a lot.'

Today, Maria still runs and for most of the year she lives happily in South Africa with her mother.

21   What is the writer trying to do in the text?

    A   persuade more Africans to take up athletics
    B   describe how Maria became a top athlete
    C   give information about Mozambique
    D   explain how Maria manages to stay fit

22   José Craveirinha found out about Maria when

    A   he went to watch a local football competition.
    B   she was blamed for her team losing a football competition.
    C   he saw an article about her role in a football match.
    D   people complained about another member of her football team.

23 When José first introduced Maria to athletics, she

A didn't know what was involved.
B was worried about being injured.
C was keen to learn everything he knew.
D didn't think her family would approve.

24 What does Maria say about the girls she met in the United States?

A They did not make full use of their abilities.
B Their training programmes were less demanding than hers.
C They did not show enough respect for the trainers.
D Their experiences of life were very different from hers.

25 What would Maria say about her life?

A
> José has made all my dreams possible. From the first day we met, I was certain I wanted to become a top athlete.

B
> My life hasn't always been easy but I've had many opportunities. Running is important to me and so is my family.

C
> I regret becoming involved in athletics. It was horrible leaving Mozambique and my parents. I'd like to go back to football.

D
> The US has some wonderful training facilities, so I'm glad that I agreed to go when I was first offered the chance.

Part 5

Questions 26–35

Read the text below and choose the correct word for each space.
For each question, mark the correct letter **A**, **B**, **C** or **D** on your answer sheet.

Example:

0	**A** made	**B** turned	**C** done	**D** put

Answer:

0	A B C D
	■ □ □ □

HONEY

Honey is a sweet liquid **(0)** .... by bees. It **(26)** .... of water and sugars. Bees may travel as **(27)** .... as seventy-five thousand kilometres and visit over two million flowers to produce just half a kilo of honey. The colour and flavour of honey depend **(28)** .... the type of flower visited. In **(29)** ...., there are more than three hundred **(30)** .... of honey.

The lighter-coloured ones are generally milder in flavour than darker honey.

In ancient **(31)** ...., honey was the main sweet food, as sugar was very **(32)** .... Honey was of great **(33)** .... to the ancient Egyptians, who used it as payment.

Today, honey is produced and eaten in **(34)** .... part of the world. Research suggests that it prevents tiredness and improves athletic performance. However, honey is not just food – it **(35)** .... be taken for sore throats and is used in many skin and hair-care products.

26	**A** involves	**B** contains	**C** includes	**D** consists
27	**A** well	**B** long	**C** soon	**D** far
28	**A** to	**B** on	**C** for	**D** with
29	**A** case	**B** order	**C** fact	**D** place
30	**A** varieties	**B** collections	**C** sets	**D** differences
31	**A** seasons	**B** times	**C** years	**D** dates
32	**A** distant	**B** rare	**C** small	**D** slim
33	**A** cost	**B** price	**C** value	**D** charge
34	**A** all	**B** some	**C** most	**D** every
35	**A** shall	**B** need	**C** can	**D** ought

WRITING

Part 1

Questions 1–5

Here are some sentences about reading books.
For each question, complete the second sentence so that it means the same as the first.
Use no more than three words.
Write only the missing words on your answer sheet.
You may use this page for any rough work.

Example:

0   I could read when I was four.

      I .... able to read since I was four.

Answer: | 0 | *have been* |

---

1   None of my friends enjoy reading as much as I do.

      I enjoy reading .... **any of my friends.**

2   I borrowed a very good book from my teacher.

      My teacher .... **me a very good book.**

3   It doesn't matter to me if a book is long or short.

      I don't .... **if a book is long or short.**

4   My mother finished *War and Peace* in only three weeks.

      It only .... **my mother three weeks to finish *War and Peace*.**

5   I am often given books as presents.

      People often .... **me books as presents.**

Part 2

Question 6

Richard, your English friend, has sent you some birthday money for you to buy a new DVD.

Write an email to Richard. In your email, you should

- thank him for the present
- tell him which DVD you are going to buy
- explain why you have chosen this film.

Write **35–45** words on your answer sheet.

Part 3

Write an answer to **one** of the questions (**7** or **8**) in this part.
Write your answer in about **100 words** on your answer sheet.
Mark the question number in the box at the top of your answer sheet.

Question 7

- This is part of a letter you receive from an English penfriend.

> My sister's getting married next week and we are
> all excited about the wedding. Tell me about
> weddings in your country. What do people wear?
> Do they eat special food?

- Now write a letter, answering your penfriend's questions.
- Write your **letter** on your answer sheet.

Question 8

- Your teacher has asked you to write a story for homework.
- Your story must begin with this sentence:

As the concert finished, I heard someone call my name.

- Write your **story** on your answer sheet.

PAPER 2   LISTENING TEST   approx 35 minutes
(including 6 minutes transfer time)

Part 1

Questions 1–7

There are seven questions in this part.
For each question there are three pictures and a short recording.
Choose the correct picture and put a tick (✓) in the box below it.

Example: Where did the man leave his camera?

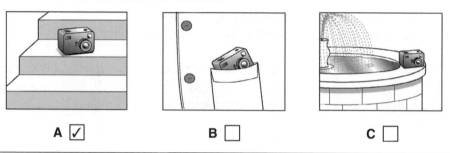

A ☑   B ☐   C ☐

---

1   Which sport will the woman learn on holiday?

A ☐   B ☐   C ☐

2   What does the girl's penfriend look like now?

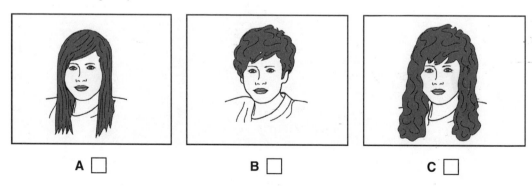

A ☐   B ☐   C ☐

3   Which animals did the children see?

A ☐ 　　　　B ☐ 　　　　C ☐

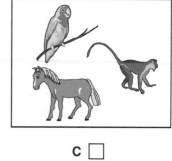

4   Which TV programme is on first?

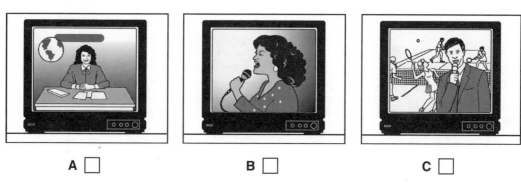

A ☐ 　　　　B ☐ 　　　　C ☐

5   What does the boy decide to buy for his grandmother?

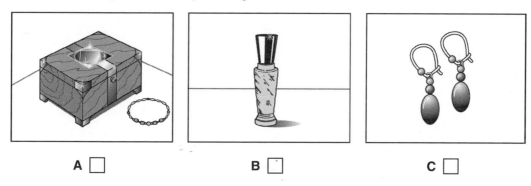

A ☐ 　　　　B ☐ 　　　　C ☐

6 What time is the man's appointment?

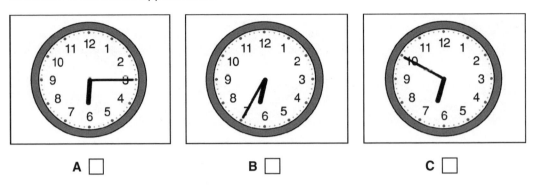

A ☐   B ☐   C ☐

7 What has the woman lost?

A ☐   B ☐   C ☐

Part 2

Questions 8–13

You will hear a man called Frank, talking on the radio about looking for ships that sank at sea long ago.

For each question, put a tick (✓) in the correct box.

---

8   The first old ship which Frank found was

    A ☐ covered by rocks.

    B ☐ older than he first thought.

    C ☐ easy to find.

9   Frank finds ships quickly because he

    A ☐ reads history books.

    B ☐ is a professional diver.

    C ☐ uses the latest equipment.

10   What does Frank say about the ship called *The Seabird*?

    A ☐ It was built in 1859.

    B ☐ It sank in a storm.

    C ☐ It was badly made.

11   Frank says his wedding ring

    A ☐ was made from gold he found himself.

    B ☐ is worth £88,000.

    C ☐ was found by a friend.

12 Frank's wife believes he should

A ☐ stop diving.

B ☐ give things to museums.

C ☐ sell some of his collection.

13 How did Frank learn to dive?

A ☐ by joining a diving club

B ☐ by going on a diving holiday

C ☐ by teaching himself

Part 3

Questions 14–19

You will hear a man telling a group of students about a trip to the theatre.
For each question, fill in the missing information in the numbered space.

Trip to Staunton Theatre

Meet at 6.00 p.m. at the **(14)** .... of the school.

The name of the play is **(15)** ....

Get a copy of the play from the **(16)** ....

Each theatre ticket will cost **(17)** £........................... .

After the theatre – have **(18)** .... and coffee.

On the return journey, the coach will stop at the
(19) .... and then the school.

Part 4

Questions 20–25

Look at the six sentences for this part.
You will hear a conversation between a teenage boy, Alex, and his sister, Rose, about where to go to eat.
Decide if each sentence is correct or incorrect.
If it is correct, put a tick (✓) in the box under **A** for **YES**. If it is not correct, put a tick (✓) in the box under **B** for **NO**.

		A YES	B NO
20	Alex and Rose's mother have gone to their Grandad's.	☐	☐
21	Alex tries to persuade Rose to cook supper.	☐	☐
22	Alex wants to eat in an expensive restaurant.	☐	☐
23	Alex likes some of the music at *Classic Express*.	☐	☐
24	Alex has eaten at *Classic Express* before.	☐	☐
25	Alex and Rose are going to walk to the restaurant together.	☐	☐

About the Speaking test

The Speaking test lasts about 10 to 12 minutes. You take the test with another candidate. There are two examiners in the room. One examiner talks to you and the other examiner listens to you. Both the examiners give you marks.

Part 1

The examiners introduce themselves and then one examiner asks you and your partner to say your names and spell them. This examiner then asks you questions about yourself, your daily life, interests, etc.

Part 2

The examiner asks you to talk about something together and gives you a drawing to help you.

Part 3

You each have a chance to talk by yourselves. The examiner gives you a colour photograph to look at and asks you to talk about it. When you have finished talking, the examiner gives your partner a different photograph to look at and to talk about.

Part 4

The examiner asks you and your partner to say more about the subject of the photographs in Part 3. You may be asked to give your opinion or to talk about something that has happened to you.

Test 3

PAPER 1   READING AND WRITING TEST   (1 hour 30 minutes)

READING

Part 1

Questions 1–5

Look at the text in each question.
What does it say?
Mark the correct letter **A**, **B** or **C** on your answer sheet.

Example:

0

A Do not leave your bicycle touching the window.

B Broken glass may damage your bicycle tyres.

C Your bicycle may not be safe here.

Answer: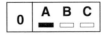

1

Photocopies have come down in price!
(Black and white only – colour copies no change)

A Some photocopies are now cheaper than they were.

B There are changes to the prices of all photocopies.

C There is no longer any colour photocopying here.

2

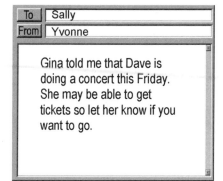

| To | Sally |
| From | Yvonne |

Gina told me that Dave is doing a concert this Friday. She may be able to get tickets so let her know if you want to go.

If Sally wants to go to the concert, she should contact

A Dave.

B Yvonne.

C Gina.

3

✤ College Office ✤

Student identity cards will be available for collection from 14 January.

A Student identity cards are unavailable after 14 January.

B The earliest students can pick up their identity cards is 14 January.

C Students should bring in their identity cards on 14 January.

4

The riding school rang. Nobody from Jane's group has booked for the midday class. For this week only, she'll have to ride at 2 o'clock instead.

A Jane should join a different riding class, because the 12 o'clock lesson is full.

B Jane must change groups, because riding classes will no longer take place at 12.

C Jane would be the only rider at 12 today, so she should come later.

5

WARNING TO MOTORISTS
Repairs to bridge start on 30/11/06
Delays likely for four weeks

A The bridge cannot be used until the end of November.

B Bridge repairs may make your journey longer from the end of November.

C Repair work on this bridge will finish in November.

Part 2

Questions 6–10

The people below all want to find a radio programme they could enjoy listening to this week.
On the opposite page there are descriptions of eight radio programmes.
Decide which programme would be the most suitable for the following people.
For questions **6–10**, mark the correct letter (**A–H**) on your answer sheet.

6  Roberta and Alice are interested in pop music. They want to listen to a live performance, and would also enjoy hearing interviews with some of the performers.

7  Paul enjoys listening to good modern drama. He works long hours during the week so he can only listen to the radio at weekends.

8  Sven teaches history and likes listening to experts talking about his subject. However, he hates shows which invite listeners to phone in.

9  Al writes poetry, and enjoys hearing other writers read their poems on the radio. He wants to have the opportunity to give his own opinions live on the programme.

10  Kim and Yannis are interested in finding out about the latest international events. They want to listen to a programme that is on every day.

Radio Programmes We Recommend This Week

A Before Our Time

On Saturday, this weekly programme includes the first part of a documentary series about the discovery of the site of a 15th-century village. Professor John Frost and his team will talk about what life was like for the villagers.

B Pop Review

This Saturday's programme discusses the very latest CD releases, so there will be a great mix of music from all over the world. This week's special report comes from Senegal.

C Good Morning

This programme has regular reports on current affairs and news stories as they happen at home and abroad, plus discussions every morning about the background to world news. All this week, the programme features interviews with ordinary people around the world who talk about the recent history of their country.

D History Team

This Wednesday, a local team tries to prove that people lived in the rocky hills of their area thousands of years ago. Specialist presenter Dr Clive Sparky describes what they find. Listeners can ring in and ask him questions, and discuss their own interests and local discoveries.

E Spotlight

This Thursday, writer Kate Dyer talks about the relationship between her poetry and her work as a history teacher. Kate will perform her latest poem, 'Sunshine'. Listeners can then phone in and talk to Kate about her work. Dramatist David Fry will also talk about his latest book on historical drama from the 19th century.

F Opinion

Find out about the news on this regular Wednesday morning programme, with a team of journalists discussing the major events of the week around the world. This week, the programme also visits the new National Library's collection of original documents from the world of literature, including internationally famous drama and poetry, with readings of some of the poems.

G Out and About

Hear all the latest in the world of pop and rock, including a week of major concerts as they happen every evening, coming direct from Birmingham. After each concert, listeners can also hear members of the band answering questions about their music.

H Showtime

This is a perfect programme for lovers of new plays, music and poetry. On Saturday, listeners have the chance to hear the prize-winning play 'Machines'. Poet Roger Brookes will also read from his new collection 'Rainbow' and composer Jack Williams will play his latest piece for classical guitar.

Part 3

Questions 11–20

Look at the sentences below about climbing Ben Nevis, a mountain in Scotland.
Read the text on the opposite page to decide if each sentence is correct or incorrect.
If it is correct, mark **A** on your answer sheet.
If it is not correct, mark **B** on your answer sheet.

11   The climbers' camp was at the bottom of Ben Nevis.

12   Their equipment was of little use on the icy snow.

13   The climbers were well prepared in case of emergency.

14   The climbers were worried by the weather forecast.

15   The whole group took regular breaks together.

16   The writer realised that he had to improve his fitness.

17   The climbers recognised the danger in taking the Tower Ridge path.

18   From the top of Ben Nevis, the climbers had a view of the sea.

19   The climbers shared the responsibility for map reading.

20   The writer began to relax when he reached the top of the mountain.

Climbing to the top of Britain

Each year thousands of people climb Ben Nevis in Scotland, and because of its northerly location, the climate can be bitterly cold. Climber Keith Hewitt describes his first time on Ben Nevis.

It was February, my first big winter climb. Our route was up the north face of the mountain to Tower Ridge. It's six hundred metres up – probably the longest climb in Britain. We planned to camp for three days in the 'Corries', which are like big bowls cut into the walls of the mountain half-way up.

We were carrying tents, sleeping bags, and metal spikes for our boots – you'd have trouble on Ben Nevis without them because you get snow so hard it's like walking on ice. Even though some of the group were very experienced, we packed all kinds of safety equipment, including lights for attracting attention, hard hats and extra clothing. Although the weather forecast was perfect, with no strong winds, there was still a general feeling of nervousness when we set out. Ben Nevis in winter is always a challenge.

The track soon climbed and my legs felt heavy. Being the weakest member of the group, I had to rest more frequently. The others sometimes stopped for a break to let me catch up, but as soon as I reached them they set off again. I promised myself that in future I would always train properly before a climb.

After 200 metres, we reached the beginning of Tower Ridge, the route that would take us to the top of Ben Nevis. It's only a metre and a half wide and the mountain drops away hundreds of metres on each side. We knew we had to keep calm and concentrate on every step as we moved slowly along it.

After seven hours of climbing, we reached the top. On a clear day, you can see the sea and right across it to the island of Skye, 48 kilometres away. However, we weren't so lucky, as a mist had come down.

On Ben Nevis, getting back down to camp can be as much of a challenge as going up. You need to be able to read a map properly – a wrong turn could lead to slopes too dangerous to go down in winter. I was glad we had decided to take it in turns to do that job. That first time, it was only when I was safe in the tent that I could say I really enjoyed the experience. But at least I made it to the top.

Part 4

Questions 21–25

Read the text and questions below.
For each question, mark the correct letter **A**, **B**, **C** or **D** on your answer sheet.

Gareth Ellis

Gareth Ellis, 13, is the youngest son of Alan, an engineer, and Kath, a nursery teacher. His older brothers work in banking and computers, but Gareth's dream was always to become a clown. Three years ago, Alan, Kath and Gareth joined the circus. 'People laugh when we tell them,' says Kath. 'But it's true. Gareth has wanted to be a clown since we took him to the circus when he was three.'

When Alan lost his job, he and Kath decided to see if they could find full-time circus jobs. They both got jobs with a famous circus and Gareth began training to become a clown. He calls himself Bippo. They travel with the circus during the summer and return home for the winter. Gareth's brothers are old enough to look after the house while they are away.

'I can't say it was easy,' says Kath. 'There was a lot to think about and organise. We only had a car and a very small caravan to sleep in, and we were leaving behind our lovely house. The only thing Gareth missed was his long, hot baths.'

'People ask about my education,' says Gareth, 'but from the beginning, wherever we go, someone has always come to teach me. I follow the same books as everyone back at school and I've got a computer. I've never fallen behind my classmates.'

And the future? 'It was a difficult decision,' says Kath, 'but there was no other way to teach Gareth about being a clown. I'm happy to say it's working, and we're enjoying it.' And Gareth? 'I'm going to be the main clown in a circus one day', he says, 'perhaps Bippo's circus.'

---

21   What is the writer trying to do in the text?

    A   describe how one family changed their lives
    B   give details about how to join the circus
    C   talk about the best way to educate a child
    D   advise what to do when you lose your job

22   What would a reader learn about Gareth from the text?

    A   He does not enjoy school work.
    B   He has a definite aim in life.
    C   He would like to be at home with his brothers.
    D   He wants to be the same as other boys.

23   Alan and Kath joined the circus because

    A   they wanted to spend time travelling in the summer.
    B   they needed money in order to buy a bigger car.
    C   their older sons needed their house for themselves.
    D   their youngest son wanted to train as a performer.

24   When they first joined the circus, Kath

    A   wanted to go back home.
    B   did not have enough to do.
    C   found things difficult.
    D   was not able to sleep properly.

25   Which postcard did Gareth write just after he joined the circus?

A

> We've just arrived and I love it already. There's lots of space for our things and I've even got my own computer.

B

> I don't miss much from home. I'm managing to do all my school work. See you in the winter.

C

> I really enjoyed meeting Bippo the Clown today, but I'm missing my school friends, and I'd love a nice hot bath.

D

> I'm learning all about the circus and how to entertain people. I also have a new school to go to.

Part 5

Questions 26–35

Read the text below and choose the correct word for each space.
For each question, mark the correct letter **A**, **B**, **C** or **D** on your answer sheet.

Example:

0   **A** was   **B** is   **C** has   **D** had

Answer: | 0 | **A B C D**
■ ▭ ▭ ▭ |

The History of Shoes

In the past, importance **(0)** .... not given to shoes being comfortable or fashionable. These early foot coverings were probably animal skins, **(26)** .... people tied round their ankles during cold **(27)** .... We still use leather today, but **(28)** .... materials such as silk, plastic, or cotton are also popular, **(29)** .... on what is in fashion.

It was only one hundred and fifty years **(30)** .... that people began to wear a different shoe on each foot. Formerly, the two shoes had been straight instead of shaped and **(31)** .... be worn on the left or the right foot. All shoes used to be made by hand, but now, **(32)** .... there are shoemakers still using their **(33)** .... skills, most shoes are now machine-made in large factories. The introduction of sewing machines **(34)** .... the shoe industry to produce large **(35)** .... of cheaper shoes for a wider range of buyers.

26	**A** who	**B** why	**C** which	**D** where
27	**A** weather	**B** climate	**C** temperature	**D** condition
28	**A** either	**B** both	**C** another	**D** other
29	**A** turning	**B** depending	**C** resting	**D** taking
30	**A** before	**B** beyond	**C** ago	**D** after
31	**A** must	**B** could	**C** ought	**D** might
32	**A** although	**B** if	**C** unless	**D** since
33	**A** typical	**B** usual	**C** model	**D** traditional
34	**A** let	**B** allowed	**C** gave	**D** got
35	**A** quantities	**B** totals	**C** sums	**D** sizes

WRITING

Part 1

Questions 1–5

Here are some sentences about a visit to an activity park.
For each question, complete the second sentence so that it means the same as the first.
Use no more than three words.
Write only the missing words on your answer sheet.
You may use this page for any rough work.

Example:

0   We had never been to the park before.

 It was .... **we had been to the park.**

Answer: | **0** | *the first time* |

---

1   The park entrance ticket was cheaper than I'd expected.

 The park entrance ticket wasn't as .... **I'd expected.**

2   A lot of people were there in spite of the rain.

 Even though it ...., **a lot of people were there.**

3   I liked the water slide best, and my brother did too.

 I liked the water slide best, and .... **did my brother.**

4   'Who does this towel belong to?' my mother asked.

 My mother asked, '... **is this towel?'**

5   We stayed until the activity park closed.

 We .... **leave until the activity park closed.**

Part 2

Question 6

A new shopping centre has opened in your town, and you are going there on Saturday.

Write an email to your English friend Rosie. In your email, you should

- invite her to visit the shopping centre with you
- explain why you want to go there
- suggest a good place to meet.

Write **35–45** words on your answer sheet.

Part 3

Write an answer to **one** of the questions (**7** or **8**) in this part.
Write your answer in about **100 words** on your answer sheet.
Mark the question number In the box at the top of your answer sheet.

Question 7

- This is part of a letter you receive from an English penfriend.

> A new gym has opened near my house. I go there
> twice a week. What sports facilities are available
> near where you live? How often do you do sport?

- Now write a letter, answering your penfriend's questions.
- Write your **letter** on your answer sheet.

Question 8

- Your English teacher has asked you to write a story.
- This is the title for your story:

The lost birthday present

- Write your **story** on your answer sheet.

PAPER 2   LISTENING TEST   approx 35 minutes
(including 6 minutes transfer time)

Part 1

Questions 1–7

There are seven questions in this part.
For each question there are three pictures and a short recording.
Choose the correct picture and put a tick (✓) in the box below it.

Example: Where did the man leave his camera?

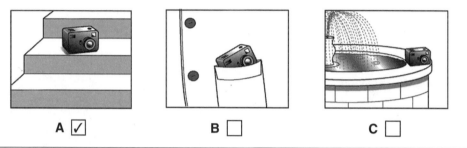

A ✓   **B** ☐   **C** ☐

---

1   What is the weather forecast for tomorrow?

A ☐   **B** ☐   **C** ☐

2   What will they buy at the supermarket?

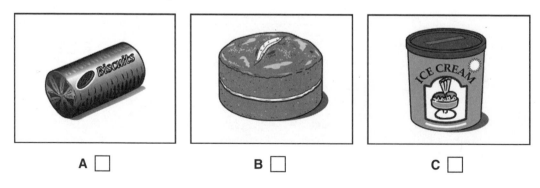

A ☐   **B** ☐   **C** ☐

3   Which T-shirt does the woman buy?

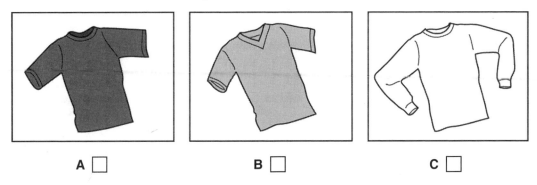

A ☐   B ☐   C ☐

4   What will the girl take with her on holiday?

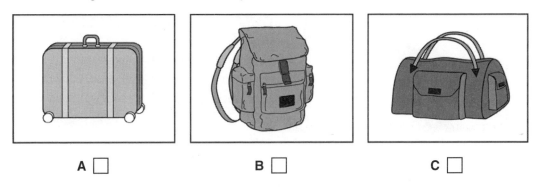

A ☐   B ☐   C ☐

5   Which exercise is the teacher describing?

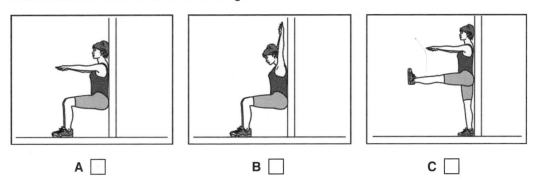

A ☐   B ☐   C ☐

6 What time will the train to London leave?

A ☐   B ☐   C ☐

7 Which sport will the boy do soon at the centre?

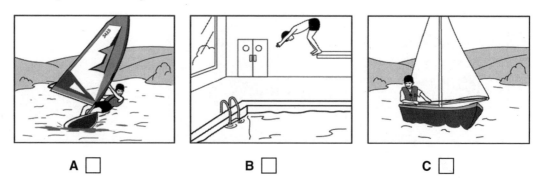

A ☐   B ☐   C ☐

Part 2

Questions 8–13

You will hear an interview with a woman called Rachel who is talking about the shows she puts on for children.

For each question, put a tick (✓) in the correct box.

8   Before her children were born, Rachel worked as

A ☐ an art teacher.

B ☐ a painter.

C ☐ an actor.

9   Who first thought of doing a show at a party?

A ☐ Rachel's husband

B ☐ Rachel's children

C ☐ Rachel's parents

10 Rachel's neighbour, Lena, helps by

A ☐ making some dolls for the shows.

B ☑ performing in the shows.

C ☐ writing the music for the shows.

11 When Rachel did a play about a lion

A ☐ the children laughed too much.

B ☐ the children were frightened.

C ☐ the children's parents complained.

12 How do Rachel's daughters help her?

A ☐ They show new dolls to their school friends.

B ☐ They think of ideas for new stories.

C ☐ They give her their opinions on her new plays.

13 Rachel thinks her shows are successful because

A ☐ she enjoys doing them so much.

B ☐ she does a show daily.

C ☐ they are suitable for all ages.

Part 3

Questions 14–19

You will hear a telephone message about a Business Studies course.
For each question, fill in the missing information in the numbered space.

Business Studies Course

Course start date :   **(14)** ....

Course begins with :   **(15)** .... *about business*

What students mustn't bring to class :   **(16)** ....

Visitors' car park :   *next to the* **(17)** ....

Language classes available :   *Spanish and* **(18)** ....

Name of Business Studies secretary :   *Sonia* **(19)** ....

Part 4

Questions 20–25

Look at the six sentences for this part.
You will hear a conversation between a student called Peter, and his father, about their plans for the summer.
Decide if each sentence is correct or incorrect.
If it is correct, put a tick (✓) in the box under **A** for **YES**. If it is not correct, put a tick (✓) in the box under **B** for **NO**.

		A YES	B NO
20	Peter's mother is planning to go to Scotland.	☐	☐
21	Peter's father hopes to have an active holiday.	☐	☐
22	Peter's father thinks Peter should have a holiday before starting work.	☐	☐
23	Peter's father will pay for everything at the campsite.	☐	☐
24	Peter has met Jim's son more than once.	☐	☐
25	Peter suggests everyone could meet before the trip to Scotland.	☐	☐

About the Speaking test

The Speaking test lasts about 10 to 12 minutes. You take the test with another candidate. There are two examiners in the room. One examiner talks to you and the other examiner listens to you. Both the examiners give you marks.

Part 1

The examiners introduce themselves and then one examiner asks you and your partner to say your names and spell them. This examiner then asks you questions about yourself, your daily life, interests, etc.

Part 2

The examiner asks you to talk about something together and gives you a drawing to help you.

Part 3

You each have a chance to talk by yourselves. The examiner gives you a colour photograph to look at and asks you to talk about it. When you have finished talking, the examiner gives your partner a different photograph to look at and to talk about.

Part 4

The examiner asks you and your partner to say more about the subject of the photographs in Part 3. You may be asked to give your opinion or to talk about something that has happened to you.

Test 4

PAPER 1 READING AND WRITING TEST (1 hour 30 minutes)

READING

Part 1

Questions 1–5

Look at the text in each question.
What does it say?
Mark the correct letter **A**, **B** or **C** on your answer sheet.

Example:

0

A Valuable objects are removed at night.

B Valuables should not be left in the van.

C This van is locked at night.

Answer:

1

To be taken between meals at six-hourly intervals, up to three times daily.

It is essential

A to wait six hours before having more of this medicine.

B to take this medicine straight after meals.

C to use this medicine more than three times a day.

2

Louise,
Suzie rang. The photo shop has lost all her photos of your trip to Vienna and she'd like copies of yours.
Mum

What should Louise do?

A take some new photos of Suzie

B give Suzie some photos

C help Suzie find her photos

3

Basketball Training

Professional coach available for pre-booked groups – 48 hours' notice required

A Basketball players are only allowed to practise here if accompanied by a professional coach.

B Basketball training for groups is cancelled until further notice.

C A basketball coach is available if a booking is made far enough in advance.

4

We're staying at the Plaza Hotel. It's not the hotel we wanted but it doesn't matter because this one is nearer the beach and I'm spending all my time there.
Sabrina

How does Sabrina feel about the Plaza Hotel?

A She's disappointed with it.

B She wishes it was nearer the beach.

C She thinks it has an advantage.

5

CHARLTON THEATRE

Book early for Swan Lake to avoid disappointment as this is a popular show.

A We regret that there are no tickets left for the early performance of Swan Lake.

B If you want to see Swan Lake, buy your tickets as soon as possible.

C Swan Lake is unfortunately cancelled due to disappointing ticket sales.

Part 2

Questions 6–10

The people below all want to buy an audiobook (a book recorded on CD).
On the opposite page there are descriptions of eight CDs.
Decide which CD would be the most suitable for the following people.
For questions **6–10**, mark the correct letter (**A–H**) on your answer sheet.

---

6  David enjoys spending time in the countryside, exploring different locations and learning about their past. He would enjoy listening to a description of somewhere that he could visit afterwards.

7  Emile enjoys classical music and drama and is interested in history. He would like to listen to a serious CD that will give information about a particular period of history.

8  Ysabelle has to drive a lot for her job. She is looking for some amusing fiction to listen to in the car and would like a story that lasts a long time.

9  Omah is studying literature at university. He is particularly interested in modern poetry and would like to hear some of the poems he knows well being read aloud.

10  Tamsin's favourite novels take place in the past, and she likes exciting stories that move fast. She would like a CD that's easy to listen to and doesn't last too long.

Books recorded on CD

A Hafiz

Hafiz was a 14th-century Persian poet, and on this audiobook his poems are read aloud to a background of instrumental music. Nataraja Kallio reads beautifully. This CD is a great introduction to the work of Hafiz.

B Skulls and Skeletons

This recording about life in the 11th century was originally a radio series. In addition to the main text, some well-known musicians play instruments from the period, and some important documents and poetry of the time are read by actors.

C Coming Home

Jane Brown decided to take a look at a house for sale near where she grew up. The beauty of the house and the scenery around it amazed her. In this audiobook, she talks about local castles and ruins and gives lots of historical information about the area.

D The Apple Tree

The Lintons' house has no water or electricity but the beautiful countryside offers them peace and quiet. But when the Dobsons move in next door, things go frighteningly wrong. If you like mystery and suspense, and have plenty of time to listen, this is the novel for you.

E Off the Page

Listening to poems is one of our most ancient traditions and many people still believe that it's as important to listen to them as it is to read them. Here you can listen to some of the best poems from the 1980s to the present day. This is a great audiobook if you are short of time, as nothing in this collection lasts very long.

F Unlucky

When Mary Moreton throws herself into the back of George Bennet's taxi, he falls instantly in love with her. However, she is already in love with someone else. Events move quickly after that and the novel is very funny. You will need several hours for this audiobook but it's great to listen to while you are busy with other jobs.

G Over the Horizon

Tim falls in love at first sight with Lily when he meets her on an 18th-century prison ship. The ship sinks, he rescues her, and they run away together. The action builds throughout the story. Listeners who enjoy historical adventure will love this book. This is not serious fiction though, and it's all over pretty quickly.

H Mother Learns to Drive

This is an amusing collection of true stories about growing up in the American countryside. In one particularly funny story, the author describes his mother learning to drive. This is a fairly long audiobook, but it is easy to listen to.

Part 3

Questions 11–20

Look at the sentences below about Tanya Streeter, a professional diver.
Read the text on the opposite page to decide if each sentence is correct or incorrect.
If it is correct, mark **A** on your answer sheet.
If it is not correct, mark **B** on your answer sheet.

---

11 Tanya Streeter's world record in 2003 was the deepest she had ever dived.

12 There were other people in the water with Tanya during her record-breaking dive.

13 Tanya accepts that free-diving can be an extremely dangerous activity.

14 Tanya's training programme depends on the event she is preparing for.

15 Most of Tanya's training takes place in the water.

16 Tanya is careful to limit the number of training dives she does in a month.

17 Tanya spends more time helping environmental organisations than appearing in advertisements.

18 Tanya's interest in the natural world started at an early age.

19 Tanya has found that being famous has its advantages.

20 Because she started free-diving fairly late, Tanya feels her sports career may be short.

Free-diving in the Caribbean

Tanya Streeter holds four world records in free-diving, the sport in which competitors reach extraordinary depths on only one breath of air.

In 2003, Tanya Streeter made history when she became the first person to dive 120 metres into the ocean while holding her breath, and come back up to the top without help. She had been deeper a year before but on that occasion she swam back up using a balloon. This time, however, she held her breath for over three and a half minutes, which made her the only female in any sport to break the world record of a man. A team of fourteen safety divers at different depths watched the dive.

Following reports of several serious accidents involving other divers, some people have complained that free-diving is too dangerous a sport, but Tanya doesn't agree, insisting that safety is the most important thing, followed closely by training.

Most free-divers concentrate on one or two types of event within the sport, but whatever Tanya is in training for, her practice timetable remains the same. Two thirds of the programme is spent doing land-based training at the gym, with the rest divided between the pool and the ocean. She uses an exercise bike to help improve the fitness of her heart. However, she doesn't run, whether outdoors or on running machines, because she doesn't want to injure her knees. Instead, she finds that fast walking is a very good way to build her fitness. When she starts doing practice dives, she generally travels away from home. She aims to do fourteen dives over a four-week period, with a rest day between each diving day. It is essential that she doesn't get tired because that could ruin all the preparation.

When Tanya is not preparing for an event, she makes frequent public appearances, mainly to advertise sports products. She has also supported environmental organisations, for example doing research projects or making films. Spending her childhood on the Caribbean island of Grand Cayman, she went swimming whenever she could, and long afternoons were spent exploring rock pools in order to watch the sea life. Tanya says that her life today is like living her childhood dreams. Because she is well-known in some countries, she thinks people are prepared to listen to her when she is talking about environmental issues.

As for the future, Tanya, who is now in her thirties, says she plans to keep breaking her own world records. As she didn't take up free-diving until she was twenty-five, Tanya is keen to stress that she doesn't intend to retire from the sport for many years to come.

Part 4

Questions 21–25

Read the text and questions below.
For each question, mark the correct letter **A**, **B**, **C** or **D** on your answer sheet.

Little Chefs

For one group of children aged between ten and fifteen, Saturdays are spent learning the art of serious cooking. Their weekly lessons in small classes are so popular that there is a waiting list of 30 children who want to do the course. Parents pay £280 for the course where their children can have fun and learn how to make good food.

Class member Bill, aged ten, says, 'I love my mum's cooking and now I can do it better than her. The teachers make us laugh, especially when we sit down with them to share the food we've made.'

Flora is twelve, and she's having problems preparing onions. 'I love cooking. I did a meal for ten friends which they really enjoyed. Then my mum suggested I take up a hobby, instead of doing nothing at weekends. I was happy staying at home, so I wasn't too keen at first. I'm really glad I decided to come, though.'

Their teacher, Philippe, says, 'It's great fun. Children pay attention and remember things better than adults, although the kitchen isn't always as tidy when they're cooking! As adults, we're always learning more about food. If parents interest their children in cooking while they are young, they'll have enough skill to make food for themselves when they leave home.'

21   What is the writer trying to do in the text?

    A   warn parents not to expect too much from their children
    B   advertise schools that teach people how to cook
    C   describe how some children spend their spare time
    D   explain why parents want to learn more about cooking

22   What can a reader find out from this text?

    A   which dishes students prefer to cook on the course
    B   why the classes are so successful
    C   how much one lesson costs
    D   when the next classes begin

23   Why did Flora join the course?

    A   Her friends persuaded her to do it.
    B   She wanted to learn to cook a big meal.
    C   She felt bored at weekends, with nothing to do.
    D   Her mother wanted her to develop an interest.

24   What does Philippe say about his young students?

    A   They will be confident about cooking in the future.
    B   They have a good memory but don't always listen.
    C   They keep the kitchen cleaner than adults do.
    D   They teach their parents what they have learnt in class.

25   What would one of Philippe's students say to a friend?

A

> We made onion soup yesterday. The course is great, although there are 30 people in my class.

B

> I go every Saturday, and now I can cook as well as my mum. I'm ten, and I'm the oldest.

C

> It's great. No one's over 15 and the food looks delicious. I just wish we could eat it together instead of taking it home.

D

> I was on a waiting list for ages, but now I'm on the course. Last week I cut up some onions – it was hard!

Part 5

Questions 26–35

Read the text below and choose the correct word for each space.
For each question, mark the correct letter **A**, **B**, **C** or **D** on your answer sheet.

Example:

0   **A** on   **B** in   **C** at   **D** to

Answer: | 0 | A B C D ▬ □ □ □ |

San Francisco

San Francisco lies **(0)** .... the coast of northern California. The earliest Europeans to discover the **(26)** .... were led by a Spanish explorer **(27)** .... name was Gaspar de Portolá.

He first saw it in 1769. Surprisingly, **(28)** .... San Francisco Bay is a wonderful natural harbour, it was discovered by land **(29)** .... than by sea.

In 1849, people **(30)** .... in San Francisco in their thousands **(31)** .... to find gold. However, it was not the men looking for the gold that got rich. The richest people **(32)** .... their money from owning banks and law firms and they built themselves large houses on one of the hills. This was **(33)** .... as Nob Hill.

Nowadays, tourists are **(34)** .... to San Francisco because there they can see famous places like Chinatown and the Golden Gate Bridge. Many even **(35)** .... the short boat trip to the island of Alcatraz to see the former prison.

26	**A** area	**B** part	**C** space	**D** position
27	**A** who	**B** whose	**C** what	**D** which
28	**A** if	**B** unless	**C** although	**D** despite
29	**A** except	**B** instead	**C** apart	**D** rather
30	**A** reached	**B** arrived	**C** entered	**D** approached
31	**A** wondering	**B** hoping	**C** considering	**D** depending
32	**A** did	**B** became	**C** made	**D** brought
33	**A** told	**B** called	**C** named	**D** known
34	**A** interested	**B** attracted	**C** pleased	**D** excited
35	**A** take	**B** spend	**C** go	**D** travel

Visual material for the Speaking test

1A

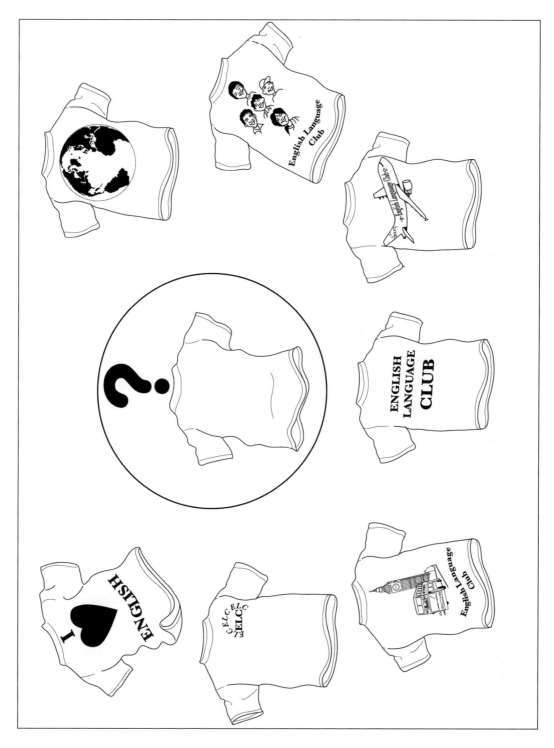

1B

2C

2A

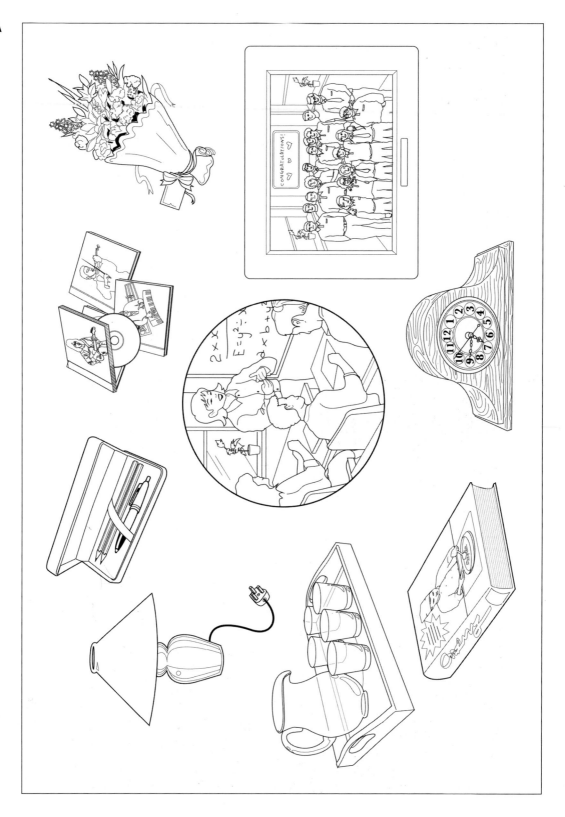

2B

1C

3A

3B

4C

4A

3C

4B

4D

WRITING

PART 1

Questions 1–5

Here are some sentences about a camping holiday.
For each question, complete the second sentence so that it means the same as the first.
Use no more than three words.
Write only the missing words on your answer sheet.
You may use this page for any rough work.

Example:

0   Sebastian had never been camping before.

   This was .... **Sebastian had been camping.**

Answer: | **0** | *the first time* |

---

1   The campsite was not far from the sea.

   The campsite was quite .... **the sea.**

2   Sebastian asked the manager where the showers were.

   Sebastian asked the manager, 'Where .... **showers?'**

3   Sebastian succeeded in putting up the tent on his own.

   Sebastian was able .... **up the tent on his own.**

4   Sebastian and his friends went swimming every day.

   Every day Sebastian went swimming and .... **did his friends.**

5   The sea was warmer than they had expected.

   The sea was not as .... **they had expected.**

PART 2

Question 6

You are going to miss your English class tomorrow.

Write a note to your English teacher. In your note, you should

- apologise for missing tomorrow's class
- explain why you can't be there
- suggest what you could do to cover the work you miss.

Write **35–45** words on your answer sheet.

Part 3

- Write an answer to **one** of the questions (**7** or **8**) in this part.
- Write your answer in about **100 words** on your answer sheet.
- Mark the question number in the box at the top of your answer sheet.

Question 7

- This is part of a letter you receive from an English penfriend.

> I've just bought some new trousers. They're black and I really like them. Tell me about the clothes you like wearing. Do you enjoy shopping for clothes?

- Now write a letter to your penfriend about clothes.
- Write your **letter** on your answer sheet.

Question 8

- Your English teacher has asked you to write a story.
- This is the title for your story:

The lost suitcase

- Write your **story** on your answer sheet.

PAPER 2   LISTENING TEST   approx 35 minutes
(including 6 minutes transfer time)

Part 1

Questions 1–7

There are seven questions in this part.
For each question there are three pictures and a short recording.
Choose the correct picture and put a tick (✓) in the box below it.

Example: Where did the man leave his camera?

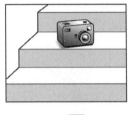  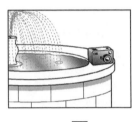

A ✓   B ☐   C ☐

---

1   Which of Miranda's things will Lucy be able to use?

A ☐   B ☐   C ☐

2   What can't the woman find?

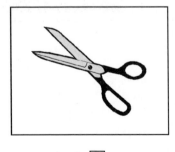  

A ☐   B ☐   C ☐

3 Which ring has the woman lost?

A ☐ B ☐ C ☐

4 What time did the girl arrive?

 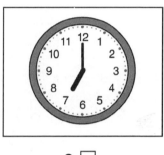

A ☐ B ☐ C ☐

5 What will be on television at 10 o'clock this evening?

A ☐ B ☐ C ☐

6 Where will the party be?

A ☐   B ☐   C ☐

7 What did the man buy?

A ☐   B ☐   C ☐

Part 2

Questions 8–13

You will hear a man called Paul Hart talking about his trip to Africa with a team of scientists. For each question, put a tick (✓) in the correct box.

8 Why did Paul choose the part of Africa he visited?

A ☐ It is good for walking.

B ☐ It will soon change.

C ☐ He had been there before.

9 What made the team's journey slow?

A ☐ clearing paths through the forest

B ☐ finding somewhere safe to camp

C ☐ carrying heavy equipment

10 What did Paul worry about during the trip?

A ☐ the number of dangerous animals

B ☐ getting the information he needed

C ☐ being responsible for a team of people

11 Paul says that the team didn't have enough food because

A ☐ some people ate more than they should.

B ☐ the walk took longer than expected.

C ☐ some of the food went bad too quickly.

12 Why were the team grateful to a fisherman they met?

A ☐ He let everyone rest on his boat.

B ☐ He helped one of them who was ill.

C ☐ He told them which direction to take.

13 How does Paul feel now he is back home?

A ☐ He is planning to do another trip.

B ☐ He misses the people in the team.

C ☐ He thinks the trip was a valuable experience.

Part 3

Questions 14–19

You will hear a woman talking about flights in a hot air balloon.
For each question, fill in the missing information in the numbered space.

Hot Air Balloon Flights

Children under 12 must be with an adult.

All passengers need to be **(14)** ....

Balloon flights are best when there are
light winds, no **(15)** .... and a clear sky.

Passengers need to wear outdoor clothes and **(16)** ....

Flights travel between 5 and 30 kilometres.

Passengers return to the airfield in a **(17)** ....

Flights are available from the month of **(18)** .... each year.

For booking and information, phone **(19)** ....
or visit www.hotairballoons.com

Part 4

Questions 20–25

Look at the six sentences for this part.
You will hear a conversation between a girl called Ella, and her father, about the school holidays.
Decide if each sentence is correct or incorrect.
If it is correct, put a tick (✓) in the box under **A** for **YES**. If it is not correct, put a tick (✓) in the box under **B** for **NO**.

		A YES	B NO
20	Ella and her father both think she has worked hard.	☐	☐
21	Ella is happy to be alone during the holidays.	☐	☐
22	Ella has a lot in common with her friends.	☐	☐
23	The family's last camping trip was unsuccessful.	☐	☐
24	Someone has asked Ella to look after a horse in the holidays.	☐	☐
25	Ella's father is keen for her to spend the holidays relaxing.	☐	☐

About the Speaking test

The Speaking test lasts about 10 to 12 minutes. You take the test with another candidate. There are two examiners in the room. One examiner talks to you and the other examiner listens to you. Both the examiners give you marks.

Part 1

The examiners introduce themselves and then one examiner asks you and your partner to say your names and spell them. This examiner then asks you questions about yourself, your daily life, interests, etc.

Part 2

The examiner asks you to talk about something together and gives you a drawing to help you.

Part 3

You each have a chance to talk by yourselves. The examiner gives you a colour photograph to look at and asks you to talk about it. When you have finished talking, the examiner gives your partner a different photograph to look at and to talk about.

Part 4

The examiner asks you and your partner to say more about the subject of the photographs in Part 3. You may be asked to give your opinion or to talk about something that has happened to you.

Frames for the Speaking test

TEST 1

Part 1 (2–3 minutes)

Tasks   Identifying oneself; giving information about oneself; talking about interests.

Phase 1
Examiner

A/B   Good morning / afternoon / evening.
Can I have your mark sheets, please?

A/B   I'm ………… and this is ………… .
He / she is just going to listen to us.

A   Now, what's your name?
Thank you.

B   And, what's your name?
Thank you.

<table>
<tr><td></td><td></td><td style="text-align:right">**Back-up prompts**</td></tr>
<tr><td>**B**</td><td>Candidate B, what's your surname?
How do you spell it?

Thank you.</td><td>How do you write your
family / second name?</td></tr>
<tr><td>**A**</td><td>And Candidate A, what's your surname?
How do you spell it?

Thank you.</td><td></td></tr>
<tr><td></td><td>*(Ask the following questions.
Ask Candidate A first.)*

Where do you live / come from?

Do you work or are you a student in . . .?
What do you do / study?

Thank you.

(Repeat for Candidate B.)</td><td>Do you live in . . .?

Have you got a job?
What job do you do? / What
subject(s) do you study?</td></tr>
</table>

Phase 2
Examiner
(Select one or more questions from the list to ask each candidate. Ask Candidate B first.)

	Back-up prompts
Do you enjoy studying English? Why (not)?	Do you like studying English?
Do you think that English will be useful for you in the future?	Will you use English in the future?
What did you do yesterday evening / last weekend?	Did you do anything yesterday evening / last weekend? What?
What do you enjoy doing in your free time?	What do you like to do in your free time?

Thank you.

(Introduction to Part 2)

In the next part, you are going to talk to each other.

Part 2 (2–3 minutes)

T-SHIRT DESIGN

Tasks   Discussing alternatives; expressing opinions; making choices.

Examiner   *Say to both candidates:*

> I'm going to describe a situation to you.
>
> The members of an English Language Club would like to have their own special T-shirt. Talk together about the different things they can put on the T-shirt and decide which one would be best.
>
> Here is a picture with some ideas to help you.

Ask both candidates to look at picture 1A on page I of the Student's Book and repeat the frame.

> I'll say that again.
>
> The members of an English Language Club would like to have their own special T-shirt. Talk together about the different things they can put on the T-shirt and decide which one would be best.
>
> All right? Talk together.

Allow the candidates enough time to complete the task without intervention. Prompt only if necessary.

Part 3 (3 minutes)

PEOPLE AND PHOTOS

Tasks Describing people and places; saying where people and things are and what different people are doing.

Examiner *Say to both candidates:*

> Now, I'd like each of you to talk on your own about something. I'm going to give each of you a picture of people and photographs.
>
> Candidate A, here is your picture. *(Ask Candidate A to look at photo 1B on page II of the Student's Book.)* Please show it to Candidate B, but I'd like you to talk about it. Candidate B, you just listen. I'll give you your picture in a moment.
>
> Candidate A, please tell us what you can see in your picture.

(Candidate A) *Approximately one minute.*
If there is a need to intervene, prompts rather than direct questions should be used.

Ask Candidate A to close his/her book.

Examiner Now, Candidate B, here is your picture. It also shows someone with photographs. *(Ask Candidate B to look at photo 1C on page IV of the Student's Book.)* Please show it to Candidate A and tell us what you can see in the picture.

(Candidate B) *Approximately one minute.*

Ask the candidates to close their books before moving to Part 4.

Part 4 (3 minutes)

Tasks Talking about one's likes and dislikes; expressing opinions.

Examiner *Say to both candidates:*

> Your pictures showed people and photographs. Now, I'd like you to talk together about the type of photographs you like to look at, and the type of photographs you like to keep.

Allow the candidates enough time to complete the task without intervention.

Prompt only if necessary.

> Thank you. That's the end of the test.

Back-up Prompts
1. Talk about the photographs you like to **look** at.
2. Talk about the photographs you like to **keep**.
3. Talk about the type of photographs you **dislike**.
4. Talk about the type of photographs you **take**.

TEST 2

Part 1 (2–3 minutes)

Tasks   Identifying oneself; giving information about oneself; talking about interests.

Phase 1
Examiner

A/B   Good morning / afternoon / evening.
Can I have your mark sheets, please?

A/B   I'm .... and this is ....
He/she is just going to listen to us.

A   Now, what's your name?
Thank you.

B   And, what's your name?
Thank you.

                                                Back-up prompts

B Candidate B, what's your surname? How do you spell it? Thank you. **A** And Candidate A, what's your surname? How do you spell it? Thank you.	How do you write your family / second name?
(Ask the following questions. *Ask Candidate A first.)* Where do you live / come from? Do you work or are you a student in . . .? What do you do / study? Thank you. *(Repeat for Candidate B.)*	Do you live in . . .? Have you got a job? What job do you do? / What subject(s) do you study?

Phase 2
Examiner

(Select one or more questions from the list to ask each candidate. Ask Candidate B first.)

	Back-up prompts
Do you enjoy studying English? Why (not)?	Do you like studying English?
Do you think that English will be useful for you in the future?	Will you use English in the future?
What did you do yesterday evening / last weekend?	Did you do anything yesterday evening / last weekend? What?
What do you enjoy doing in your free time?	What do you like to do in your free time?

Thank you.

(Introduction to Part 2)

In the next part, you are going to talk to each other.

Part 2 (2–3 minutes)

WEDDING PRESENT

Tasks   Discussing alternatives; expressing opinions; making choices.

Examiner   *Say to both candidates:*

> I'm going to describe a situation to you.
>
> A school teacher is getting married next month. Her class would like to give her a present. Talk together about the different presents her class could give her, and say which would be best.
>
> Here is a picture with some ideas to help you.

Ask both candidates to look at picture 2A on page III of the Student's Book and repeat the frame.

> I'll say that again.
>
> A schoolteacher is getting married next month. Her class would like to give her a present. Talk together about the different presents her class could give her, and say which would be best.
>
> All right? Talk together.

Allow the candidates enough time to complete the task without intervention. Prompt only if necessary.

Part 3 (3 minutes)

WEATHER

Tasks   Describing people and places; saying where people and things are and what different people are doing.

Examiner   *Say to both candidates:*

> Now, I'd like each of you to talk on your own about something. I'm going to give each of you a photograph of people enjoying different kinds of weather.
>
> Candidate A, here is your photograph. *(Ask Candidate A to look at photo 2B on page IV of the Student's Book.)* Please show it to Candidate B, but I'd like you to talk about it. Candidate B, you just listen. I'll give you your photograph in a moment.
>
> Candidate A, please tell us what you can see in your photograph.

(Candidate A)   *Approximately one minute.*
If there is a need to intervene, prompts rather than direct questions should be used.

Ask Candidate A to close his/her book.

Examiner   Now, Candidate B, here is your photograph. It also shows people enjoying different kinds of weather. *(Ask Candidate B to look at photo 2C on page II of the Student's Book.)* Please show it to Candidate A and tell us what you can see in the photograph.

(Candidate B)   *Approximately one minute.*

Ask the candidates to close their books before moving to Part 4.

Part 4 (3 minutes)

Tasks   Talking about one's likes and dislikes; expressing opinions.

Examiner   *Say to both candidates:*

> Your photographs showed people enjoying different kinds of weather. Now, I'd like you to talk together about the type of weather you prefer and say what you enjoy doing in different types of weather.

Allow the candidates enough time to complete the task without intervention.
Prompt only if necessary.

Thank you. That's the end of the test.

Back-up Prompts
1. Talk about the type of weather you **like**.
2. Talk about the type of weather you **don't like**.
3. Talk about what you do when it is **hot / wet / cold**.
4. Talk about where you **go** in hot / wet / cold weather.

TEST 3

Part 1 (2–3 minutes)

Tasks   Identifying oneself; giving information about oneself; talking about interests.

Phase 1
Examiner

A/B   Good morning / afternoon / evening.
Can I have your mark sheets, please?

A/B   I'm ………… and this is ………… .
He / she is just going to listen to us.

A   Now, what's your name?
Thank you.

B   And, what's your name?
Thank you.

Back-up prompts

B
Candidate B, what's your surname? How do you spell it? Thank you.

How do you write your family / second name?

A
And Candidate A, what's your surname? How do you spell it? Thank you.

(Ask the following questions. Ask Candidate A first.) Where do you live / come from? Do you work or are you a student in . . .? What do you do / study? Thank you. *(Repeat for Candidate B.)*

Do you live in . . .? Have you got a job? What job do you do? / What subject(s) do you study?

Phase 2
Examiner

(Select one or more questions from the list to ask each candidate. Ask Candidate B first.)

Back-up prompts

Do you enjoy studying English? Why (not)?

Do you like studying English?

Do you think that English will be useful for you in the future?

Will you use English in the future?

What did you do yesterday evening / last weekend?

Did you do anything yesterday evening / last weekend? What?

What do you enjoy doing in your free time?

What do you like to do in your free time?

Thank you.

(Introduction to Part 2)

In the next part, you are going to talk to each other.

Part 2 (2–3 minutes)

BEACH HOLIDAY

Tasks Discussing alternatives; expressing opinions; making choices.

Examiner *Say to both candidates:*

> I'm going to describe a situation to you.
>
> A friend is going on a seaside holiday, but she doesn't like sitting on the beach all day. Talk together about the different things your friend can do at the seaside and say which would be most enjoyable.
>
> Here is a picture with some ideas to help you.

Ask both candidates to look at picture 3A on page V of the Student's Book and repeat the frame.

> I'll say that again.
>
> A friend is going on a seaside holiday, but she doesn't like sitting on the beach all day. Talk together about the different things your friend can do at the seaside and say which would be most enjoyable.
>
> All right? Talk together.

Allow the candidates enough time to complete the task without intervention. Prompt only if necessary.

Part 3 (3 minutes)

AT WORK

Tasks   Describing people and places; saying where people and things are and what different people are doing.

Examiner *Say to both candidates:*

> Now, I'd like each of you to talk on your own about something. I'm going to give each of you a photograph of someone at work.
>
> Candidate A, here is your photograph. *(Ask Candidate A to look at photo 3B on page VI of the Student's Book.)* Please show it to Candidate B, but I'd like you to talk about it. Candidate B, you just listen. I'll give you your photograph in a moment.
>
> Candidate A, please tell us what you can see in your photograph.

(Candidate A) *Approximately one minute.*

      If there is a need to intervene, prompts rather than direct questions should be used.

      Ask Candidate A to close his/her book.

Examiner Now, Candidate B, here is your photograph. It also shows someone at work. *(Ask Candidate B to look at photo 3C on page VIII of the Student's Book.)* Please show it to Candidate A and tell us what you can see in the photograph.

(Candidate B) Approximately one minute.

      Ask the candidates to close their books before moving to Part 4.

Part 4 (3 minutes)

Tasks   Talking about one's likes and dislikes; expressing opinions.

Examiner *Say to both candidates:*

> Your photographs showed people at work. Now, I'd like you to talk together about the type of place where you would like to work and what would be good about it.

Allow the candidates enough time to complete the task without intervention.
Prompt only if necessary.

Thank you. That's the end of the test.

Back-up Prompts
1. Talk about places where you'd **like** to work.
2. Talk about what would be **good / bad** about it.
3. Talk about places where you **wouldn't** like to work.
4. Talk about places where your **friends** / members of your **family** work.

100

TEST 4

Part 1 (2–3 minutes)

Tasks   Identifying oneself; giving information about oneself; talking about interests.

Phase 1
Examiner

A/B   Good morning / afternoon / evening.
Can I have your mark sheets, please?

A/B   I'm ………… and this is ………… .
He / she is just going to listen to us.

A   Now, what's your name?
Thank you.

B   And, what's your name?
Thank you.

Back-up prompts

B
Candidate B, what's your surname? How do you spell it? Thank you.

How do you write your family / second name?

A
And Candidate A, what's your surname? How do you spell it? Thank you.

(Ask the following questions. *Ask Candidate A first.)* Where do you live / come from? Do you work or are you a student in . . .? What do you do / study? Thank you. *(Repeat for Candidate B.)*

Do you live in . . .? Have you got a job? What job do you do? / What subject(s) do you study?

Phase 2
Examiner
(Select one or more questions from the list to ask each candidate. Ask Candidate B first.)

	Back-up prompts
Do you enjoy studying English? Why (not)?	Do you like studying English?
Do you think that English will be useful for you in the future?	Will you use English in the future?
What did you do yesterday evening / last weekend?	Did you do anything yesterday evening / last weekend? What?
What do you enjoy doing in your free time?	What do you like to do in your free time?

Thank you.

(Introduction to Part 2)

In the next part, you are going to talk to each other.

Part 2 (2–3 minutes)

PICNIC

Tasks   Discussing alternatives; expressing opinions; making choices.

> SUITABLE FOR GROUPS OF THREE AND PAIRS

Examiner   *Say to both / all candidates:*

> I'm going to describe a situation to you.
> A group of friends has prepared a picnic but they aren't sure where to eat it. Talk together about the different places they can go for a picnic, and then say which would be best.
> Here is a picture with some ideas to help you.

Ask both/all candidates to look at picture 4A on page VII of the Student's Book and repeat the frame.

> I'll say that again.
> A group of friends has prepared a picnic but they aren't sure where to eat it. Talk together about the different places they can go for a picnic, and then say which would be best.
> All right? Talk together.

Allow the candidates enough time to complete the task without intervention. Prompt only if necessary.

Part 3 (3 minutes)

HOMES

Tasks   Describing people and places; saying where people and things are and what different people are doing.

Examiner	*Say to both / all candidates:*

> Now, I'd like each of you to talk on your own about something. I'm going to give each of you a photograph of people in their homes.
>
> Candidate A, here is your photograph. *(Ask Candidate A to look at photo 4B on page VIII of the Student's Book.)* Please show it to Candidate(s) B (and C), but I'd like you to talk about it. Candidate(s) B (and C), you just listen. I'll give you your photographs in a moment.
>
> Candidate A, please tell us what you can see in your photograph.

(Candidate A) *Approximately one minute.*

If there is a need to intervene, prompts rather than direct questions should be used.

Ask Candidate A to close his/her book.

Examiner

> Now, Candidate B, here is your photograph. It also shows people in their home. *(Ask Candidate B to look at photo 4C on page VI of the Student's Book.)* Please show it to Candidate(s) A (and C) and tell us what you can see in the photograph.

(Candidate B) *Approximately one minute.*

Ask the candidates to close their books before moving to Part 4.

Examiner

> Now, Candidate C, here is your photograph. It also shows people in their home. (Ask Candidate C to look at photo 4D on page VIII of the Student's Book.) Please show it to Candidates A and B and tell us what you can see in the photograph.

(Candidate C) *Approximately one minute.*

Ask the candidates to close their books before moving to Part 4.

Part 4 (3 minutes)

Tasks   Talking about one's likes and dislikes; expressing opinions.

Examiner   *Say to both / all candidates:*

> Your photographs showed people in their homes. Now, I'd like you to talk together about the things you like to do when you are at home, when you are alone and when you are with other people.

Allow the candidates enough time to complete the task without intervention.
Prompt only if necessary.

> Thank you. That's the end of the test.

Back-up Prompts
1. Talk about the things you like to do at **home**.
2. Talk about what you like to do **alone / with other people**.
3. Talk about the **people** you spend time with at home.
4. Talk about times when you prefer to **go out**.

Key

Test 1

READING

Part 1

1 C   2 B   3 B   4 A   5 C

Part 2

6 E   7 C   8 D   9 B   10 G

Part 3

11 A   12 A   13 A   14 B   15 B   16 B   17 A   18 A
19 B   20 B

Part 4

21 B   22 C   23 D   24 C   25 A

Part 5

26 D   27 C   28 A   29 A   30 B   31 D   32 C   33 A
34 B   35 A

WRITING

Part 1

1 Are you
2 permitted/allowed/able/authorised
3 wear (your) OR be wearing (your)
4 more popular
5 big/large enough

Part 2

Task-specific Mark Scheme

The content elements that need to be covered are:

i   explanation of why candidate needs the bicycle
ii information about how long candidate will need the bicycle
iii details of when candidate will return the bicycle

The following sample answers can be used as a guide when marking.

SAMPLE A (Test 1, Question 6: Email to Sam)

Hello Sam, How are you? I want to give me a favor. I want to borrow you bicycle because you know that I like all about it and I don't have a bicycle. I will need it for only 5 day. Please I really need it, as soon I finished I will return it, ok? Please I need your answer. Bye take care kisses.

Examiner Comments

One content point has been omitted – the candidate doesn't really say why he/she needs the bicycle.

Mark: 3

SAMPLE B (Test 1, Question 6: Email to Sam)

Hello Sam,
I hope you well!
I am writing this email to you because I want to borrow your bicycle. My girlfriend and I are going to spend next weekend on the lake. And we want to travel around the lake by bicycles. Unfortunately, I have only one. Could you give the bicycle for the weekend? I'll bring it back to you on Monday morning.
Thank you.

Examiner Comments

All content points are covered, and the message is clearly communicated.

Mark: 5

SAMPLE C (Test 1, Question 6: Email to Sam)

> Hi, sam
> I lik To borrow me your picycle for five dayes because I'll go to cantery sid with may family so I will be back to you after five days.

Examiner Comments

Two content elements are unsuccessfully dealt with and this message is hard to follow.

Mark: 2

Part 3

The following sample answers can be used as a guide when marking.

SAMPLE D (Test 1, Question 7: Letter to a friend)

> Hi John!
> How are you and, your family? What are you doing now? Do you have a job? What are you doing in your free time?
>   I'm fine, thank you very much. I'm working at the moment, I'm writting you in my office. My favourite restaurant is with a good servis, good meals, romantic, and clean, it's very important for me if it is clean. In my town, we have a restaurant, the name is Strada we can eat italian food, pasta, pizza, good salad etc... But I would like to visit the new restaurant in yout town, I think it's very nice! Telle me when we can meet for a good dinner. We can inveted another friends to have a good evening. I hope everythings are ok for you?
> All whiches!
> See you soon!

Examiner Comments

This is an adequate attempt at the task, with ambitious but slightly flawed language, which means some effort is required by the reader. There is an adequate range of structures and vocabulary, e.g. 'My favourite restaurant . . . if it is clean'. There is some attempt at organisation and there are a number of non-impeding errors, e.g. 'servis', 'it's very important for me if it is clean'.

Band: 3

SAMPLE E (Test 1, Question 7: Letter to a friend)

Dear Eleonora,

Many thanks for your letter, it was really nice to hear from you again. It's such a long time since we wrote to each other.

In your letter, you aksed me if I had a favourite restaurant.

In my town, which is called Tours, we have lots of restaurants. But the name of my favourite restaurant is "La Trattoria".

It's an Italian restaurant, which is situated in the oldest quarter where everyone goes to have a drink, but it's mostly frequented by students. I like this restaurant because we can have italian food but also typical food from my area like cheese, foie gras (duck paté). The atmosphere is very pleasant because there is a soft music and the people who work there, are very friendly.

If you come in Tours, we will go to have a meal. I am sure you will love this restaurant.

Give my regards to your family. I look forward to seeing you soon.

Love

Examiner Comments

This is a very good attempt with confident and ambitious use of language, e.g. 'It's an Italian restaurant . . . frequented by students'. The letter contains a wide range of structures and vocabulary, e.g. 'the atmosphere is very pleasant', 'the people who work there, are very friendly' and is well organised with simple linking. There are a few minor errors, e.g. 'a soft music', but these are non-impeding, and no effort is required by the reader.

Band: 5

SAMPLE F (Test 1, Question 7: Letter to a friend)

As you know I really like the hungarian food., so it is no question, where is my favourit restaurant in Budapest. Hungarian kitchen is quite spicey, but in my opinion, this fact made the Hungarian food well knowed all around the world. I like particularly one on the Danube's bank, where the sight is so butufoul. You can enjoy the panorama of the Gelleit mountain, the Palace, and you can see the most famous bridge, the Chain-bridge as well. The service of this restaurnat is very friendly, or as I used to saying: very "hungarian". The food is fantastic, the waiters are very helpfuly, so you can get there everything, if you want to have such a nice evening. Even if you are going there with your girlfriend, you can spent a romantic time together, and I am sure, she would be very pleased.

Examiner Comments

This is a good attempt, using fairly ambitious language with reasonable fluency, e.g. 'You can enjoy the panorama of the Gelleit mountain . . . Chain-bridge as well'. There is a more than adequate range of structure and vocabulary and appropriate linking. There are a number of errors, e.g. 'well knowed', 'butufoul', 'the waiters are very helpfuly', but they are non-impeding so only a little effort is required by the reader.

Band: 4

SAMPLE G **(Test 1, Question 8: I was on the beach . . .)**

> I was on the beach when my mobile phone rang I saw
> that may batery is low & I didn't pick up the phone.
> On the beach I read book and I went to pub I finished
> me beer and I went to home about 6 p.m. I opened my
> windows and I went to slep at 10 p.m. To-day I will
> go to cimema in the evning with my friends. But in the
> morning car hit me and now I'm in the hospital I can
> took that why I witering thos story so I'm realy sory but
> I'll not come to school in next week beacuase I'm not
> able. This is realy story from my life.

Examiner Comments

This is a poor attempt, which is difficult to understand at times, due to an incoherent sequence which leads to confusion and also numerous impeding errors, e.g. 'I can took that why I witering thos story'.

Band: 2

SAMPLE H (Test 1, Question 8: I was on the beach . . .)

I was on the beach when my mobile phone rnag. It was my flatmate. She was very nervous and anxious. She told me that while we were having holidays somebody came inside our flat. And he had stolen our computer and some cash! I was furious. So I went to home immediately. Our flat was in a mess. It was disaster! Both of us were crying. We phoned to the police office, half an hour later polices arrived. They asked something to us, but neither of us didn't know anything. Police man said to us, "Don't be afraid and worried about it". But we weren't able to like that. But 2 days later I was able to get the phone from police. The man who has stolen our computer was caught. He was a man who lived next door of us. Eventually we were able to bring back our computer and the man apologized us and moved another flat.

Examiner Comments

This is a good attempt with fairly ambitious use of language, but in the second half the ambition is flawed, which prevents the script getting a higher mark, e.g. 'They asked something . . . know anything'. The range is more than adequate and there is evidence of organisation, e.g. 'but', '2 days later', 'eventually'. There are some errors, although generally non-impeding, e.g. 'the man apologized us' and only a little effort is required from the reader.

Band: 4

SAMPLE I (Test 1, Question 8: I was on the beach . . .)

I was on the beach when my mobile phone rang. I looked at the mobile screen but the number was unknown. I deceded to answer anyway. "Hello!" I said. "Hello, Mr Tandulkar, this is the manager of the "Brooke" restaurant. I wanted you to know that the reservation of your table is confirmed at nine o'clock, this evening." "What?" I asked. "I don't have any reservation, and I didn't call you for booking any table for this evening!". "I'm sorry Mr Tandulkar but I have a reservation at your name, a woman called this morning and she booked a table for two". I was curious to meet that unknown woman, so I went to the restaurant at nine o'clock dressed on my best suit. The manager brought me to the mysterious woman and I was anxious to meet her! I looked at her and I was stunned! It was my sister! What a surprise. She wanted to celebrate her birthday! We had a very nice evening but at last I've paid the bill!

Examiner Comments

This is a very good attempt with confident and ambitious use of direct speech, e.g. 'What?' I asked. 'I don't have any reservation ...'. There is a more than adequate range within a well organised story, with beginning, middle and end. There are some minor errors which are non-impeding, e.g. 'at last I've paid the bill', 'dressed on my best suit' and no effort is required from the reader.

Band: 5

PAPER 2   LISTENING

Part 1

1 B   2 B   3 C   4 B   5 A   6 A   7 A

Part 2

8 A   9 C   10 B   11 B   12 C   13 A

Part 3

14   artist/painter
15   6th (of) November
16   18/eighteen
17   hotel(s)
18   elephant(s)
19   lunch

Part 4

20 B   21 B   22 A   23 B   24 A   25 B

Test 1 transcript

This is the Cambridge Preliminary English Test, Test 1. There are four parts to the test. You will hear each part twice.

For each part of the test, there will be time for you to look through the questions and time for you to check your answers.

Write your answers on the question paper. You will have six minutes at the end of the test to copy your answers onto the answer sheet.

The recording will now be stopped. Please ask any questions now, because you must not speak during the test.

[pause]

Now open your question paper and look at Part 1.

PART 1   *There are seven questions in this part. For each question there are three pictures and a short recording. Choose the correct picture and put a tick in the box below it.*

Before we start, here is an example.

Where is the girl's hat?

Woman: Where's your new hat, Sally? I hope you haven't left it on the school bus.

Girl: Don't worry, Mum. I put it in my school bag because I was too hot.

Woman: Are you sure? I can't see it there. You probably dropped it in the road somewhere.

Girl: Oh, here it is – hanging in the hall. I forgot to take it this morning.

[pause]

The first picture is correct so there is a tick in box A.

Look at the three pictures for Question 1 now.

[pause]

Now we are ready to start. Listen carefully. You will hear each recording twice.

One. What was damaged in the storm?

Man: Was the roof of your house all right after the storm, Anna? I saw a workman there with a ladder today.

Woman: I'd had the roof repaired recently so that wasn't a problem. The workman was putting some new glass in an upstairs window. I think a branch from a tree broke it when it fell off in the wind. I was quite lucky – it didn't damage my car which was parked right under the tree.

[pause]

Now listen again.

[The recording is repeated.]

[pause]

Two. What present does the man decide to take?

Man: My boss has invited me to dinner at his house tomorrow night, but I don't know what sort of present I should take.

Woman: I suppose flowers are best, but it's not a good time of year for them . . . and people always take chocolates; that's really boring. What about a plant?

Man: I think I'd be happier with the boring chocolates than with a plant actually, but thanks for the ideas, anyway.

[pause]

Now listen again.

[The recording is repeated.]

[pause]

Three. Which is the woman's jacket?

Woman: Excuse me, has anyone found my jacket? I left it on the plane. It's grey, with two buttons down the front and one on each sleeve.

Man: Anything in the pockets, madam?

Woman: I don't think so.

Man: Yes, I've got it here.

[pause]

Now listen again.

[The recording is repeated.]

[pause]

Four. Which sport is <u>not</u> included in the price of the holiday?

Man: Hello. This is the travel agency returning your call. You left a message about the holiday you've booked, asking which sports are included in the cost. There is an extra charge for windsurfing but if you want to play golf, that's free for all hotel guests and horse-riding is also available at no extra charge, which is good because I think you were especially interested in that. Let me know if I can help you with any other information. Goodbye.

[pause]

Now listen again.

[The recording is repeated.]

[pause]

Five. Which postcard will they send?

Woman: We mustn't forget to send Mum a postcard . . . how about this one with a picture of a castle?

Man: Well, it's nice, but it's *not* where we're actually staying. What about a view of the beach and town instead? Or perhaps one of the garden pictures if you think she'd prefer it. Look at the cottage and all the flowers . . .

Woman: Mmm . . . I think your first idea was better . . . we could put a cross to show where we're staying.

Man: Right then, let's do that.

[pause]

Now listen again.

[The recording is repeated.]

[pause]

Six. Where do they decide to go?

Woman: So, we've got three hours free. Shall we go to an exhibition? What do you think?

Man: Well, there's an exhibition of photographs at the city museum, or there's a sculpture exhibition at the art gallery, which is meant to be good.

Woman: Oh, sculpture's boring! Let's go to the museum. I like photos, and we haven't been there since last year when they had that really interesting exhibition of clothes. Do you remember?

Man: OK. I can go and see the sculptures another day.

[pause]

Now listen again.

[The recording is repeated.]

[pause]

Seven. What will the boy do first?

Boy: I'm off now, Mum. I'm going to meet Ben at the tennis club because he's bought some new handlebars for his bike and he wants me to help him put them on . . . and I've got to go to the library to take my books back sometime today too.

Woman: Well, do that before you start work on the bike because it isn't open this afternoon.

Boy: OK. And we're going to play tennis after we've done the bike, so I won't see you until supper this evening. Bye!

[pause]

Now listen again.

[The recording is repeated.]

[pause]

That is the end of Part 1.

[pause]

PART 2   *Now turn to Part 2, questions 8–13.*

You will hear an English woman called Britta talking to an interviewer about her life in Berlin, the capital of Germany.

For each question, put a tick in the correct box. You now have 45 seconds to look at the questions for Part 2.

[pause]

Now we are ready to start. Listen carefully. You will hear the recording twice.

Man: Britta, you're English, but you live in Berlin. Have you lived here for a long time?

Woman: Well, I was born in England, but I've lived in Germany for the past twenty years. I arrived in Berlin about four years ago. Before that, I lived in Bonn for six years, but I work as a journalist, and when the newspaper moved to Berlin, I moved with them.

Man: Were you pleased to come to Berlin?

Woman: Yes, I was. I was looking forward to being in a big city like Berlin. Bonn was quite a lot smaller, so I love the busy atmosphere and all the cultural entertainments here: museums, theatres and so on. The only thing I don't like is the traffic; it's a bit noisy in the mornings. It wakes me up about 6.30, but most days I have to get up early anyway!

Man: Where do you live in Berlin?

Woman: I have a flat in the old part of the city. It's right in the centre, and it's not too expensive – it costs me about £500 a month. My street is becoming very popular: there are lots of new art galleries, and small cafés and friendly restaurants everywhere. Eating out in Berlin is fun, and it's cheap, so it's something I do quite often.

Man: How do you find transport in Berlin?

Woman: Well, the transport system here is very good, so I have a tram and bus ticket, but in fact, most of the time I cycle. Travel here is much cheaper than in other countries I know – perhaps that's why people don't walk very much!

Man: What do you like to do in Berlin at the weekends?

Woman: Well, I like art, so sometimes I go to one of the galleries. I have a nephew called Philippe. He's only three but he likes coming with me. He likes the café best, I think. And it's a change from going to the park – that's something he does very often. He usually comes out with me while his parents go shopping.

Man: Do you miss your friends and family in England?

Woman: I don't really miss England – most of my friends are here. I don't see much of my work colleagues socially, but I've got some very good friends who live in the same street as me. I enjoy meeting people, and I find Berlin is a very friendly city.

Man: Thank you for talking to us, Britta.

[pause]

Now listen again.

[The recording is repeated.]

That is the end of Part 2.

[pause]

PART 3   *Now turn to Part 3, questions 14–19.*

You will hear a man called Stephen Mills talking to a group of people about a trip to India to see tigers.

For each question, fill in the missing information in the numbered space. You now have 20 seconds to look at Part 3.

[pause]

Now we are ready to start. Listen carefully. You will hear the recording twice.

Man: Hello. I'm Stephen Mills. I will travel with you on the Tiger Tour to India, but I'm not your tour guide. I work as an artist and I'm going to take some photographs of tigers so that I can use them when I paint some pictures later. An expert guide will join the group when we arrive in India, but I'm leading the group until then.

　　　We leave London on the 6th of November, arriving in India the following day. It's a good time of year to visit the wildlife park where the tigers live. The rainy season finishes in October. And later in the year, the park gets more crowded and the tigers become shy.

　　　We'll spend ten days in the wildlife park. There are twenty other types of animal and three hundred types of bird to see as well as tigers. There are eighteen of us altogether and everything is organised for our comfort by the tour company. For example, although we're in the jungle, we won't have to sleep in tents! The hotels where we'll stay are all very comfortable.

　　　To be sure of seeing tigers, we'll stay in two different parts of the wildlife park. We'll spend three days in the north, where we'll travel around in an open truck, and the rest of the time in the south, where we'll travel around on elephants. That should be fun!

　　　On the way back to London, we have dinner and one night's bed and breakfast in the Indian capital, Delhi. There you can either go sightseeing or go shopping, whichever you prefer. But please note that lunch is not provided on our day of departure, as the plane leaves at two in the afternoon.

　　　Now, if there are any questions . . .

[pause]

Now listen again.

[The recording is repeated.]

That is the end of Part 3.

[pause]

Key

PART 4

Now turn to Part 4, questions 20–25.

Look at the six sentences for this part. You will hear a conversation between a boy, Carl, and a girl, Susanna, about a school concert.

Decide if each sentence is correct or incorrect. If it is correct, put a tick in the box under A for YES. If it is not correct, put a tick in the box under B for NO. You now have 20 seconds to look at the questions for Part 4.

[pause]

Now we are ready to start. Listen carefully. You will hear the recording twice.

Boy: Hi Susanna, I'm just going to the practice for the school concert. Are you coming to play your violin in the school orchestra?

Girl: I'm afraid not, Carl. I'm not at all keen on playing in concerts.

Boy: You're not nervous about performing in front of an audience, are you?

Girl: It's not that, but there are lots of other things I'd rather be doing.

Boy: But I thought you liked music. You have violin lessons, don't you?

Girl: Yes I do, but I don't enjoy them. The worst part is having to practise for half an hour every day. I never get any better and it just seems a waste of time.

Boy: Oh, I enjoy practising because then I feel that I'm making progress. In fact, playing the piano is a way of escaping from the stress of my school work.

Girl: I'd be happy if I could stop my violin lessons, but my parents won't let me. They say I'll regret it later, but I don't agree. It's not as if I'm going to make music my career like you are.

Boy: I'm not good enough to be a professional musician, I'm afraid. And it's much too uncertain. I'm hoping to be a chemist, like my father – that offers much more security!

Girl: I want a good career too, but I don't want to be a teacher like my parents. Perhaps when I've been to university I'll have more idea of what I want to do. I'll probably get a job abroad, because I'd really love to travel and see the world.

Boy: Well, there's lots of time to decide. But what about this concert – they really need more violins in the orchestra – won't you come and join in?

Girl: Sorry, you can't make me change my mind.

Boy: Well, that's a pity – I suppose you won't want a ticket to the concert either.

Girl: You're right, but I hope it goes well!

[pause]

Now listen again.

[The recording is repeated.]

That is the end of Part 4.

[pause]

You now have six minutes to check and copy your answers onto the answer sheet.

Note: Teacher, stop the recording here and time six minutes. Remind students when there is **one** minute remaining.

That is the end of the test.

Test 2

PAPER 1   READING AND WRITING

READING

Part 1
1 B   2 B   3 A   4 C   5 C

Part 2
6 D   7 B   8 E   9 G   10 F

Part 3
11 A   12 A   13 B   14 A   15 A   16 B   17 B   18 A   19 B
20 A

Part 4
21 B   22 C   23 A   24 D   25 B

Part 5
26 D   27 D   28 B   29 C   30 A   31 B   32 B   33 C   34 D
35 C

WRITING

Part 1
1 (much) more than
2 (has) lent
3 mind/care/worry
4 took
5 give

Part 2

Task-specific Mark Scheme
The content elements that need to be covered are:

i   thanks (to friend) for the present/birthday money
ii details of which DVD candidate is intending to buy
iii explanation of why candidate has chosen the particular DVD

The following sample answers can be used as a guide when marking.

Key

SAMPLE A (Test 2, Question 6: Email to Richard)

> Dear Richard
> I write to thank you for the present. I'm very happy that you give me the DVD of "Spiderman 2" because I hadn't it. This afternoon I'm going to buy for you the DVD of "The GLADIATOR". I chose it because I like very much and because it is my favourite film.

Examiner Comments

This answer implies a misreading of the question; point 1 is acceptable but points 2 and 3 are irrelevant.

Mark: 2

SAMPLE B (Test 2, Question 6: Email to Richard)

> Hi Richard!
> Thanks for the money! I'm very happy. I will buy a DVD. Do you remember the first film we have seen together? I'll buy it! I remember very good moments that I have passed with you when I see it that I will never forget. Bye!

Examiner Comments

This is a clever reading of the question! The answer is complete.

Mark: 5

SAMPLE C (Test 2, Question 6: Email to Richard)

> Dear Richard
> Hello Richard. How are you? I really thank you for the present you sent
> me. With the money you sent me I'm going to buy the new DVD "NARNIA"
> because it's a fantastic film and very scared. It's the best!
> Love
> [signature]

Examiner Comments

All content elements have been adequately dealt with and the message has been communicated successfully on the whole.

Mark: 4

SAMPLE D (Test 2, Question 7: Letter to a penfriend)

> Dear Jenny,
> How are you? I hope fine. Thanks a lot for your letter. It is wonderful that
> your sister is getting married. What a suprise! Well, I think all weddings are
> quite diffrent, but I can remember when my aunt got married 2 years ago. It
> was in the summer and of course all guest looked very summery. They all had
> diffrent types of dresses and suits. I saw lots of red, yellow and orange
> colours. It was amazing. They had also diffrent kinds of food because not
> everybody eats the same food. There was fish, meat, soups, diffrent kinds of
> salats and vegetables. I hope you will enjoy the wedding. Have a nice
> celebration. Good luck for your sister. I hope to hear from you soon.
> Love,
> [signature]

Examiner Comments

This is a very good attempt with confident and ambitious use of language, e.g.: 'Well, I think all weddings are quite diffrent . . .'. There is a wide range of structures and vocabulary and some simple linking devices have been used, e.g.: 'because', 'and', with evidence of organisation, e.g.: 'in the summer' and '2 years ago'. There are some minor non-impeding errors, e.g.: 'suprise', 'diffrent' and 'salats' but no effort is required from the reader.

Band: 5

SAMPLE E (Test 2, Question 7: Letter to a penfriend)

Dear Sue!

I am so excited because my sister getting married next Saturday. My all family getting ready. In my country the weddings are very interesting. The bride wearing a white big dress till midnight after she change her dress for a red, short dress. The husband wearing a black suit. Usually the wedding starts about at 4pm and finish the next morning about 5 am. A food is always traditional hungarian. On the wedding we having a fun and we danceing a lots. I hope one day you will see what a hungarian wedding. Tell me what's happening on the English wedding.

Lots of love

Examiner Comments

This is an adequate attempt with a suitable range of structures and vocabulary, e.g.: 'Usually the wedding starts about at 4pm', 'change her dress for' and 'traditional'. The narrative has some cohesion and there are a number of non-impeding errors, e.g.: 'My all family getting ready' and 'On the wedding we having a fun' so only a little effort is required from the reader.

Band: 3

SAMPLE F (Test 2, Question 7: Letter to a penfriend)

Dear, Sally

How are you? Thank you for your letter and condratulion for your sister. I'm dont hear hear that well you want know for weding in my country. We are making a bigger celebration and we invitied a many friends on the day. We are wearing a drees wedding. it was special for it. The women how weding is wearing a beatiful wedding semiler than you and she make her hair a new stely. In the end of day bring the food. We have a much food and different kind of the food becouse we invited many people.

I hope to invited you for medding my brother next manth.

I am looking fowrawd to seeing your soon.

Love

[signature]

Examiner Comments

This is an inadequate attempt with severe flaws, leading to incoherence, e.g.: 'I'm don't hear hear that' and 'The women how weding is wearing'. The language is severely inaccurate – see above examples – so considerable effort is required from the reader.

Band: 2

SAMPLE G (Test 2, Question 8: As the concert finished . . .)

> As the concert finished, I heard someone call my name. I turned around and I saw a man is waving to me.
> 'Hey, Jack!' I shouted. He ran to me and looked so excited. 'I thought that was you but I'm not sure, I called your name and you turned around,' He said. 'I can't believe we can meet here' . . .
> We were very good friends since primary school but he left after we graduated and have not seen each other till now. He invited me to his wedding as he is going to marry with her girlfriend soon. He is a very famous businessman now and being very successful.
> Looking forward to go to his wedding and hope they can be sweet forever.

Examiner Comments

This is a good attempt with a fairly ambitious use of language, e.g.: ' "Hey, Jack!" I shouted. He ran to me and looked so excited.' A more than adequate range of structures and vocabulary has been used, e.g.: We were very good friends . . . graduated' within a well-organised narrative, with clear sequencing. There are some errors, generally non-impeding, e.g.: 'I thought that was you but I'm not sure'. This answer requires only a little effort from the reader.

Band: 4

SAMPLE H (Test 2, Question 8: As the concert finished . . .)

> As the concert finished, I heard someone call my name. I can't belive. It was Mark. He plays in the drumbs. We didn't see each other long time. We went together to the night school and traveled a lot of different place. He was my best friend. He lived near me. After when we finish night school he disapirt. He didn't send to me any information. I was disapointed. That concert change us life again. We meet each other, He remember also how I look. That meeting make us friendshipp again. I'm happy that I have a very cleever friend.

Examiner Comments

This is an adequate attempt overall, but flawed when ambition is attempted, e.g.: 'That meeting make us friendshipp again'. There is some attempt at organisation, but linking is not always maintained, e.g.: 'I can't belive. It was Mark. He plays in the drumbs.' There are a number of errors, mostly non-impeding, e.g.: 'We didn't see each other long time' and 'That concert change us life again'. This script requires some effort from the reader.

Band: 3

SAMPLE I (Test 2, Question 8: As the concert finished . . .)

> As the concert finished, I heard someone call my name. It was my best
> friend Pedra! We haven't seen each other for ages. I couldn't recognise her.
> She changed a lot. She looked just perfect. We decided to go to find some
> quiet place where we could have a nice talk. We went to mine house, I made
> a cup of coffee and prepared some nibbles. We were talking about school,
> remembering all our boyfriends, all the naughty things that we used to do,
> about work that we found after school and lots of more. We didn't even
> realize it was almost 3 a.m! We would talk until the morning! What a pity
> we had to say good night. But never mind. We met up next day again.

Examiner Comments

This is a very good attempt with ambitious use of language, e.g.: 'We decided to go to find some
quiet place where we could have a nice talk' and 'We were talking about . . . remembering all our
boyfriends, all the naughty things that we used to do . . .'. Very good vocabulary has been used,
e.g.: 'prepared some nibbles', 'recognise', 'never mind' and 'just perfect' in a generally well-
organised narrative, with some linking of sentences. There are a few non-impeding errors, e.g.:
'mine house', 'we would talk until the morning' and 'lots of more' but no effort is required from the
reader.

Band: 5

PAPER 2   LISTENING

Part 1

1 C   2 B   3 C   4 B   5 A   6 B   7 B

Part 2

8 C   9 C   10 B   11 A   12 C   13 A

Part 3

14   back gate
15   The Party
16   (school) secretary
17   £15.75
18   ice cream
19   bus station or bus stop

Part 4

20 B   21 B   22 A   23 A   24 B   25 A

Test 2 transcript

This is the Cambridge Preliminary English Test, Test 2. There are four parts to the test. You will hear each part twice.

For each part of the test, there will be time for you to look through the questions and time for you to check your answers.

Write your answers on the question paper. You will have six minutes at the end of the test to copy your answers onto the answer sheet.

The recording will now be stopped. Please ask any questions now, because you must not speak during the test.

[pause]

Now open your question paper and look at Part 1.

PART 1   *There are seven questions in this part. For each question there are three pictures and a short recording. Choose the correct picture and put a tick in the box below it.*

Before we start, here is an example.

Where did the man leave his camera?

Man: Oh no! I haven't got my camera!

Woman: But you used it just now to take a photograph of the fountain.

Man: Oh I remember, I put it down on the steps while I put my coat on.

Woman: Well, let's drive back quickly – it might still be there.

[pause]

The first picture is correct so there is a tick in box A.

Look at the three pictures for Question 1 now.

[pause]

Now we are ready to start. Listen carefully. You will hear each recording twice.

One. Which sport will the woman learn on holiday?

Man: . . . So if you're interested in water sports, this hotel has two pools, diving boards, and its own private beach. You can learn to water ski there, and guests can windsurf too – although the hotel advises beginners to take a few lessons before going out on their own.

Woman: Good. I'm quite a strong swimmer, and I have always wanted to try windsurfing, so that would suit me fine. I tried water skiing once, but I didn't like it.

Man: Well, I'm sure you'll enjoy your stay there then.

Woman: Good.

[pause]

Now listen again.

[The recording is repeated.]

[pause]

Two. What does the girl's penfriend look like now?

Woman: Look at these photos of my penfriend and her family. I took them during the trip.

Man: So is she the one with long hair?

Woman: Oh, that's her sister. This is her, next to me. She looks a lot like her sister, though, doesn't she? And they used to have hair the same length, but hers has always been curly. It's a shame she had it cut, though – I think it looked better when it was long.

[pause]

Now listen again.

[The recording is repeated.]

[pause]

Three. Which animals did the children see?

Woman: Well, the zoo was a bit disappointing. The children enjoyed feeding the horses and watching the monkeys and the birds, but they hoped to see lions and tigers, and there weren't any. Someone told us they don't have them there because the security isn't good enough, but I don't know if that's true.

[pause]

Now listen again.

[The recording is repeated.]

[pause]

Four. Which TV programme is on first?

Woman: . . . and welcome to our Tuesday evening programmes. At 9.00 we'll have the first of our new programmes on sport, and today you can see live the final of the international tennis cup. But before that we have singer, Jane Shelley in concert. She will perform songs from her new CD. This will be followed by today's news from around the world . . .

[pause]

Now listen again.

[The recording is repeated.]

[pause]

Five. What does the boy decide to buy for his grandmother?

Boy: My mum says I've got to buy my granny a present because she always gets me one when <u>she</u> goes on holiday. I thought I'd get her a black T-shirt.

Girl: Don't be silly, old ladies don't wear T-shirts. Why not get her some of the local perfume. It smells of roses, or one of those little wooden boxes – they're great for keeping earrings and stuff in.

Boy: That's a good idea. She does a lot of travelling, so she can use it to put her jewellery in.

[pause]

Now listen again.

[The recording is repeated.]

[pause]

Six. What time is the man's appointment?

Woman: Hello. Appointments.

Man: Hello. Could I make an appointment to see Dr. Smith, next Tuesday please? Early evening, if possible – anything after 6 o'clock.

Woman: Well, we open at 6.15 on Tuesday evenings, and there's an appointment at 6.35 or 6.50.

Man: Thanks. I'll take the earlier one. My name's . . .

[pause]

Now listen again.

[The recording is repeated.]

[pause]

Seven. What has the woman lost?

Woman: Excuse me, I was sitting over there ten minutes ago making a call on my mobile phone. I got a pen out of my bag to write something down and I think my purse fell out. I can't find it now. Has anyone handed it to you?

[pause]

Now listen again.

[The recording is repeated.]

[pause]

That is the end of Part 1.

[pause]

PART 2   *Now turn to Part 2, questions 8–13.*

You will hear a man called Frank, talking on the radio about looking for ships that sank at sea long ago.

For each question, put a tick in the correct box. You now have 45 seconds to look at the questions for Part 2.

[pause]

Now we are ready to start. Listen carefully. You will hear the recording twice.

Woman: Frank, tell us about some of the ships you've discovered.

Man: Well, there's nothing quite like finding your first old ship – it was 300 years old. It was just lying at the bottom of the sea, so it wasn't difficult to find. Most are covered in sand and rocks – but this one wasn't.

I'm actually a teacher, not a full-time diver – I dive in my free time but I often get to them before the professional divers, because I have good up-to-date equipment. Another thing that helps is talking to fishermen who tell me about their local area. I've even written a book about some of their experiences.

At the moment, I'm looking for the gold from a ship called *The Seabird*. It was an enormous well-built ship and it was coming from Australia on a winter night in 1859. Everything was going fine until the ship reached the English coast, when it crashed into some rocks in a very strong wind and sank to the bottom of the sea. It was carrying gold from Australia, and most of it is still at the bottom of the sea.

My wedding ring is actually made from gold which I found on an eighteenth-century sailing ship. A friend of mine, another diver, has already found £88,000 worth of gold from different ships. He's now decided to give up his job and become a full-time diver.

My house is full of things like coins, bottles and old guns. My wife is always complaining about the number of objects around the house – she says I should open an antiques shop – but I love all these old things. Anyway, in the end, I gave some things from my collection to museums, because I didn't want to sell them. But my wife still wasn't very pleased, I'm afraid.

As diving is a dangerous hobby, it's not a good idea to try to teach yourself. I'd advise anyone interested to do what I did. There are some excellent diving clubs like the one I joined, which run courses for beginners. It is best to do one of these before you go on a diving holiday . . .

[pause]

Now listen again.

[The recording is repeated.]

That is the end of Part 2.

[pause]

PART 3   *Now turn to Part 3, questions 14–19.*

You will hear a man telling a group of students about a trip to the theatre.

For each question, fill in the missing information in the numbered space. You now have 20 seconds to look at Part 3.

[pause]

Now we are ready to start. Listen carefully. You will hear the recording twice.

Man: Okay everyone, now I need to say a few things about our visit to Staunton Theatre next Tuesday. You need to be here at school at six o'clock. We'll meet by the back gate because the coach can't stop at the front one. We can't leave any later than six, as the play starts at 7.30.

　　　We're seeing a very interesting play called *The Party* by Andrew McVitie. It's a comedy about a birthday celebration. His works can be difficult to understand so you need to read the play in advance. There is a copy for everybody which you can pick up from the school secretary. Do that as soon as you can.

　　　I'll hand out the theatre tickets on the coach. We're all sitting together, in rows E and F. The full price of these tickets is £18, but you're lucky, because I managed to get a discount for the group, so you only have to pay £15.75 each. Could you let me have this money before Tuesday, please, and £3.50 for the coach.

　　　Now, a lot of you have suggested going somewhere together afterwards. Well, the coach driver is willing to come back a bit later, but there isn't time for a three course meal, so we'll go to a café I know nearby for an ice cream and a coffee. Don't forget to bring some money for that.

　　　I've arranged for the coach to make an extra stop before it comes back to the school. So for those of you who need to take the bus home, it will be possible for you to get off at the bus station. If you decide to take a taxi, you should find plenty of taxis there, or you can walk to the main square.

　　　Right, any questions. . .

[pause]

Now listen again.

[The recording is repeated.]

That is the end of Part 3.

[pause]

PART 4   *Now turn to Part 4, questions 20–25.*

Look at the six sentences for this part. You will hear a conversation between a teenage boy, Alex, and his sister, Rose, about where to go to eat.

Decide if each sentence is correct or incorrect. If it is correct, put a tick in the box under A for YES. If it is not correct, put a tick in the box under B for NO. You now have 20 seconds to look at the questions for Part 4.

[pause]

Now we are ready to start. Listen carefully. You will hear the recording twice.

Girl: Hi Alex, where's Mum?

Boy: She's gone out.

Girl: Has she? Where's she gone?

Boy: I don't know actually. She just left a note. I expect she's gone to Grandad's.

Girl: But Grandad's gone to his club today. He always goes on Tuesdays.

Boy: Oh yes, you're right. I don't know where she is then.

Girl: Oh, never mind. What's for supper, then?

Boy: Boring soup and boring salad.

Girl: Oh no. I could make something more interesting.

Boy: That's a good idea, but you're an awful cook, Rose. And anyway, there's nothing else in the fridge.

Girl: Let's eat out then.

Boy: We can't. I haven't got any money.

Girl: Well, I have.

Boy: Great! Let's go to the Pizza Palace!

Girl: I'm not that rich! Be reasonable, the prices at Pizza Palace are much higher than anywhere else. Why don't we go to MacGregor's?

Boy: MacGregor's! I'd rather have soup and salad at home.

Girl: The food's not that bad there. But they don't have any music.

Boy: Well, they do, but it's really awful.

Girl: They have good music at Classic Express though, don't they?

Boy: Well, sometimes they have terrible classical stuff, but you can ask them to change the CD for some cool rock music.

Girl: Oh, I've never thought of doing that. That's a good idea.

Boy: Shall we go there then? What's the food like? I've been there a few times, but only for a coffee.

Girl: Well, you'd like it. You get really huge plates of food. There would even be enough for you. I'm surprised you haven't noticed.

Boy: Well, I haven't.

Girl: Anyway, I'm hungry now. Are we going or aren't we?

Boy: Sure. Let's go by bike.

Girl: You're crazy, Alex, it's pouring with rain out there!

Boy: OK, how about a taxi?

Girl: Yes, Alex, we could take a taxi, but then I wouldn't have enough money for the meal. I'm going on foot, and you're coming with me.

Boy: Oh, all right. Sisters!

[pause]

Now listen again.

[The recording is repeated.]

That is the end of Part 4.

[pause]

You now have six minutes to check and copy your answers onto the answer sheet.

Note: Teacher, stop the recording here and time six minutes. Remind students when there is **one** minute remaining.

That is the end of the test.

Test 3

PAPER 1 READING AND WRITING

READING

Part 1

1 A   2 C   3 B   4 C   5 B

Part 2

6 G   7 H   8 A   9 E   10 C

Part 3

11 B   12 B   13 A   14 B   15 B   16 A   17 A   18 B   19 A
20 B

Part 4

21 A   22 B   23 D   24 C   25 B

Part 5

26 C   27 A   28 D   29 B   30 C   31 B   32 A   33 D   34 B
35 A

WRITING

Part 1

1   expensive/much/dear as
2   was raining/rainy/wet (weather) // rained
3   so
4   Whose
5   didn't/did not

Part 2

Task-specific Mark Scheme

The content elements that need to be covered are:

i   invitation to friend to go to shopping centre
ii reason why candidate wants to go there
iii suggestion about where to meet

The following sample answers can be used as a guide when marking.

SAMPLE A **(Test 3, Question 6: Email to Rosie)**

> Dear Rosie,
>
> I want to invite you to a new shopping centre where I want to buy some new cloth. Why don't we meet outside the restaurant which is next to my house.
>
> See you soon,
>
> [signature]

Examiner Comments

This answer is concise and complete, therefore deserves a 5.

Mark: 5

SAMPLE B **(Test 3, Question 6: Email to Rosie)**

> Dear Rosie,
>
> Hi!, Well, I'm gonna to be direct. Can you come to visit the shopping centre with me? I want to go to the shopping centre because I want a short. We can meet at my home.
>
> Bye,
>
> [signature]

Examiner Comments

All content elements have been adequately dealt with and the message has been communicated successfully, on the whole.

Mark: 4

SAMPLE C (Test 3, Question 6: Email to Rosie)

> DEAR ROSIE,
> I'M SENDING YOU THIS EMAIL BECAUSE I WANT TO INVITE YOU TO
> THE OPENING OF A NEW SHOPPING CENTRE IN MY TOWN.
> I KNOW THAT WILL BE AN OFERT IN THE OPENING. CAME TO MY
> HOUSE ON SATURDAY AT MIDDAY.
> KISSES,
> [signature]

Examiner Comments

This answer receives a lower mark as points 2 and 3 are missing.

Mark: 2

SAMPLE D (Test 3, Question 7: Letter to a penfriend)

> Hello. How are you?
> It is a problem because I think that you will have to speak with your family.
> Other problem is how much money do you pay for go and practice sports.
> Near my house I do a lot of sports but the sports that I practice very much are
> football, basketball and beisball but when I go to the gim I play machines for I will
> have a strong muscles and resistant in the legs.
> If I go to the gim and after I will go to play football I finished the day very tired.
> One day I go to the gim and the next day I go to play sports.
> With the resistant that I could have after the gim and I could be very good for the
> sports that I do the next day.

Examiner Comments

An adequate attempt with ambitious but flawed language, e.g.: 'Near my house . . . resistant in the legs'. There is an adequate range of structures and vocabulary, e.g.: 'If I go to the gim . . .', 'muscles', 'resistant' in a quite well organised letter, with simple linking, e.g.: 'but', 'when', 'after'. However, there are a number of errors, mostly non-impeding, e.g.: 'If I go to the gim and after I will go to play football I finished the day very tired'. Some effort is required from the reader.

Band: 3

SAMPLE E (Test 3, Question 7: Letter to a penfriend)

Dear Luke,

Hi. I hope you're well. I am so glad to hear from you. It's nice to know that you go to the gym regularly. I believe it will make you fit. I can't wait to see the result of your exercise. Well, near my house there are four tennis courts which open every day at nine in the morning and close at ten in the evening. It costs £10.00 for two hours. There is also a basketball court and two football fields but I have no idea how much the rent is. I heard that there is also a swimming pool being renovated at the moment right beside the tennis courts. On Saturdays, I play badminton with my cousin for about an hour, after that I get really tired. Sometimes I like to play football but unfortunately, most members of the teams are boys so it's enough for me to just watch them play. Perhaps I will go swimming as well when the pool is finished. Hope you will write again soon. Take care.

Love,

[signature]

Examiner Comments

This is a very good attempt with a wide range of structures, e.g.: 'I heard that there is also a swimming pool being renovated at the moment right beside the tennis courts', and vocabulary, e.g.: 'I can't wait to see the result'. The narrative is well organised with simple linking, e.g.: 'On Saturdays', 'sometimes'. There is a natural flow to the letter, e.g.: 'Well, near my house . . .' and errors are very minor; word choice only, i.e. 'unfortunately' and 'rent'. No effort is required from the reader.

Band: 5

SAMPLE F (Test 3, Question 7: Letter to a penfriend)

> I have been next in my house 6pm.
> No twece a week.
> Playing tennis and exercice. I like going to the beach very nice in my country is beautiful places and restaurants, museum, show the sings and very nice academic sports and exercice aerobic, music. But I like playing football. I like my brother participle in the playing football in very fast, next my house in Putney.

Examiner Comments

This is a poor effort showing a restricted command of language with little evidence of basic sentence structure, e.g.: 'show the sings . . . aerobic, music'. However, occasional phrases do make sense, e.g.: 'I like going to . . .', 'I like playing . . .'. There are numerous errors which lead to incoherence, e.g.: 'But I like playing football . . . my house in Putney'. The text requires excessive effort from the reader.

Band: 1

SAMPLE G (Test 3, Question 8: The lost birthday present)

> Jane was excited because next day was going to be her birthday! She was so happy because their parents bought her a piano and she love play it. They hide it under the stairs, and they said to Jane that she can't open it until her birthday. She couldn't wait so she dicided to go the night before her birthday and play it. When she opened the door of the room where the piano was she saw that it wasn't there. She was so worried so she went to bed again. Next day when she woke up she saw the piano in her room, and her mom was near it. She told Jane that she moved the piano because she knew she was going to play it. Ouf!

Examiner Comments

This is a good attempt with a fairly ambitious use of language. There is a more than adequate range of structures and vocabulary, e.g.: 'When she opened the door of the room where the piano was she saw that it wasn't there' with some evidence of organisation and some linking of sentences. There are some errors, mainly in tenses, e.g.: '. . . she love play it. They hide it under the stairs' but, on the whole, only a little effort is required from the reader.

Band: 4

SAMPLE H **(Test 3, Question 8: The lost birthday present)**

The lost birthday present

Hello, Emily!

I just wont to tell you what happened exactly last saturday!

Me and my friend went to the shop, because we are wont to bay a lovely Tshirt for my nice friend Zoe. We are went one of the shop in Oxford street, and the noder. Finally we are found a very famous in the street and we wher very happy and bougth a lovely, pink Tshort! We left to the shop was nearly close time. And we catch the bus and travelled back home both together. End of the bus stadion we can't find the lovely present. Probably we lose it on the bus because was very busy. Doesn't felt very happy we where realised what had happened! See you soon! All the best

[signature]

Examiner Comments

This is an inadequate attempt which starts with some ambition (e.g.: 'I just want to tell you . . . last saturday') but rapidly becomes incoherent (e.g.: 'Finally we are found . . .'). The text appears to follow a narrative sequence but is difficult to understand due to language errors, which are numerous and sometimes impede. Considerable effort is required from the reader.

Band: 2

SAMPLE I (Test 3, Question 8: The lost birthday present)

> Last month, it was my mother's birthday. My brother, my dad and I prepared an amazing party with all her friends. It was hard to organise but we did it . . . Dad told me I was in charge of the present which was a new digital camera. I put it in my room, under my pillow, thought it was a safety place . . .
>
> On the day, when my dad asked me to go and get the present, I couldn't find it! Mum was waiting, all her friends were too . . . They were all looking at me with this horrible look which means 'You've done something wrong'.
>
> After a while, mum started laughing, we didn't understand why . . . she said: 'Is the present a digital camera?!' My brother replied 'Yes, it is! How do you know?'
>
> She laughed more and more and declared that she found it in my room and she had started already to use it!
>
> We were all laughing and smiling, glad about this revelation.

Examiner Comments

This is a very good attempt with a confident and ambitious use of language, e.g.: 'Dad told me I was in charge of the present which was a new digital camera'. There is a wide range of structures and vocabulary, e.g.: 'She laughed more and more and declared that . . .', '. . . glad about this revelation' and the narrative is well organised with effective use of linking devices, e.g.: 'On the day . . .', 'After a while . . .'. There are a few minor errors which do not impede, e.g.: 'a safety place' and no effort is required from the reader.

Band: 5

PAPER 2   LISTENING

Part 1

1 C   2 A   3 A   4 B   5 A   6 C   7 C

Part 2

8 B   9 A   10 B   11 B   12 C   13 A

Part 3

14   12^(th) (of) June
15   video/film
16   (mobile) phone
17   entrance
18   Italian
19   Ashleigh

Part 4

20 B   21 A   22 A   23 B   24 B   25 A

Test 3 transcript

This is the Cambridge Preliminary English Test, Test 3. There are four parts to the test. You will hear each part twice.

For each part of the test, there will be time for you to look through the questions and time for you to check your answers.

Write your answers on the question paper. You will have six minutes at the end of the test to copy your answers onto the answer sheet.

The recording will now be stopped. Please ask any questions now, because you must not speak during the test.

[pause]

Now open your question paper and look at Part 1.

PART 1   *There are seven questions in this part. For each question there are three pictures and a short recording. Choose the correct picture and put a tick in the box below it.*

Before we start, here is an example.

Where did the man leave his camera?

Man: Oh no! I haven't got my camera!

Woman: But you used it just now to take a photograph of the fountain.

Man: Oh I remember, I put it down on the steps while I put my coat on.

Woman: Well, let's drive back quickly – it might still be there.

[pause]

The first picture is correct so there is a tick in box A.

Look at the three pictures for question 1 now.

[pause]

Now we are ready to start. Listen carefully. You will hear each recording twice.

One. What is the weather forecast for tomorrow?

Man: And now for the weather. As we go through today, the temperature will slowly rise, and the snow we've had for the last few days will disappear by the end of the afternoon. Tomorrow we can expect some rain, but by the end of the week, some sunny weather is likely.

[pause]

Now listen again.

[The recording is repeated.]

[pause]

Two. What will they buy at the supermarket?

Woman: Look, Kate, there are some of those biscuits you like!

Girl: Oh, yes. Mmm . . . they're a bit expensive, though, Mum. Why don't we have this cake instead? Remember we've got guests coming tomorrow.

Woman: Oh, I haven't forgotten. I've already made a cake, and I've bought lots of ice cream for the children.

Girl: Well, I suppose the biscuits would be nice with ice cream. Let's see . . . oh, good. I've got enough money in my purse.

[pause]

Now listen again.

[The recording is repeated.]

[pause]

Three. Which T-shirt does the woman buy?

Woman: I'd like to buy a white T-shirt with short sleeves, please. Large size.

Man: I'm afraid the white ones have long sleeves, but we've got short sleeves in the darker colours. Do you want a round neck or a V-neck?

Woman: It must be round neck. Let me think . . . umm, OK, I'll take one of the short-sleeved ones – the colour's not so important really.

[pause]

Now listen again.

[The recording is repeated.]

[pause]

Four. What will the girl take with her on holiday?

Man: Have you packed for your holiday?

Woman: No, I need to go shopping before I can do that. Last holiday, my suitcase handle got broken, so I need something that's better quality this time. But suitcases are so heavy to carry.

Man: I always take a big sports bag – it's light, and not expensive, so it doesn't matter if it gets torn.

Woman: Yes, I thought about one of those, but you need something stronger when it's going on a plane. I'll get something I can put on my back – you can carry more that way.

[pause]

Now listen again.

[The recording is repeated.]

[pause]

Five. Which exercise is the teacher describing?

Woman: OK everybody. This next exercise is a bit difficult, but it's really good for your legs. All you do is put your back against the wall . . . place your feet about half a metre away from the wall . . . move your back down the wall, so your knees are bent at 90 degrees. Now put your hands out straight in front of you . . . right . . . make sure your head is against the wall. Now, see how long you can stay like that! If you do two minutes, you're doing well.

[pause]

Now listen again.

[The recording is repeated.]

[pause]

Six. What time will the train to London leave?

Man: The train arriving at platform six is the 4.45 from London. The train due to arrive at platform four in approximately five minutes is the delayed 4.30 train to London. This train will now depart at 4.50 and travel non-stop. We apologise to passengers for the delay. Refreshments will not be available on this train.

[pause]

Now listen again.

[The recording is repeated.]

[pause]

Seven. Which sport will the boy do soon at the centre?

Boy: Have you been to the new watersports centre yet?

Girl: Oh yes, it's brilliant. There are two indoor pools, one for diving and one for swimming, and you can also have sailing lessons on the lake.

Boy: That's what I'm doing there next weekend, actually. I was hoping to take windsurfing lessons, but the leaflet says they're not starting those until next year.

[pause]

Now listen again.

[The recording is repeated.]

[pause]

That is the end of Part 1.

[pause]

PART 2   *Now turn to Part 2, questions 8–13.*

You will hear an interview with a woman called Rachel who is talking about the shows she puts on for children.

For each question, put a tick in the correct box. You now have 45 seconds to look at the questions for Part 2.

[pause]

Now we are ready to start. Listen carefully. You will hear the recording twice.

Man: Rachel, tell us how your shows for children started. You studied art at college, didn't you?

Woman: That's right. But I gave up my career as an artist when my twin daughters were born. Painting took up too much time when I was looking after them. I thought about teaching art classes part-time, but instead I started making dolls for my daughters. I love acting, so I often invented little plays for the dolls, doing the voices myself.

Man: And when did you start doing shows for other people?

Woman: When our daughters were five, my husband suggested using the dolls to entertain the children at their birthday party. I wrote a little show and he built a dolls' theatre. My daughters and their friends loved it. As a result, other parents asked me to come and do the show at their children's parties. That's how it all began.

Man: It must be a lot of work for you?

Woman: Yes. I love making the dolls, but I decided that I needed someone to help me with the shows. Luckily my neighbour, Lena, was keen to perform with me. Her husband records the music to go with the shows. It would be impossible to do everything on my own.

Man: Have you ever had any problems?

Woman: Only once. I did a show for a group of three-year-olds, and I'd written a story about a lion. Unfortunately, the children were really afraid of the lion and started crying. I was worried the parents might complain, but luckily they were all able to laugh about it afterwards.

Man: And what did you learn from that?

Woman: The experience taught me that I had to find out beforehand just what children enjoy. Like me, Lena has two daughters, so whenever we've invented a new story, we show it to our four girls first. They always tell us exactly what they think of it. And sometimes I take new dolls to the local primary school to check that children like them.

Man: And the shows continue to be successful?

Woman: They do. I have a range of different shows for five to nine-year-olds. In fact, the shows have become so successful I could do one every day, but I don't want to do that. The reason the shows have become popular, I think, is because I love every minute of every show, and so other people love them too. I certainly didn't realise when I organised that birthday party for my daughters all those years ago that it would change my life so much!

[pause]

Now listen again.

[The recording is repeated.]

That is the end of Part 2.

[pause]

PART 3   *Now turn to Part 3, questions 14–19.*

You will hear a telephone message about a Business Studies course.

For each question, fill in the missing information in the numbered space. You now have 20 seconds to look at Part 3.

[pause]

Now we are ready to start. Listen carefully. You will hear the recording twice.

Woman: Hello, this is Greenhill College. I'm leaving this message in answer to your enquiry about the Business Studies course. Firstly, you asked when the course starts. It begins on the 12th of June, and finishes four weeks later on the 7th of July. According to your letter, you're free at this time, so I hope those dates will be all right.

    At the beginning of the course, there are no lectures because we spend time watching business videos. So you won't need to bring anything for the class, as everything is provided. Don't forget, however, that although you can bring your own laptop if you wish, mobile phones are not allowed in the classroom. I'm afraid these can disturb the classes, so they've now been banned.

    You said you're coming by car. Well, as it's only a short course, you can use the visitors' car park which is just beside the main entrance. We're only a short walk away. Just turn right after the science and technology centre, cross the staff car park, and you'll see the door to the Business Studies Department in front of you.

    Finally, you also wanted to know if it's possible to attend a language course while you are here. Well, the answer is yes, but we only have room on our Italian classes. Oh, no actually . . . there's one place on the Spanish course too. We usually offer French and Japanese as well, but there aren't enough students for those classes this summer.

    So, I think that's all. But if you need to ask any further questions, please call Sonia Ashleigh – that's spelt A-S-H-L-E-I-G-H. She's the secretary in the Business Studies department, and she'll be happy to help. Thank you for your enquiry.

[pause]

Now listen again.

[The recording is repeated.]

That is the end of Part 3.

[pause]

Key

PART 4   *Now turn to Part 4, questions 20–25.*

Look at the six sentences for this part. You will hear a conversation between a student called Peter, and his father, about their plans for the summer.

Decide if each sentence is correct or incorrect. If it is correct, put a tick in the box under A for YES. If it is not correct, put a tick in the box under B for NO. You now have 20 seconds to look at the questions for Part 4.

[pause]

Now we are ready to start. Listen carefully. You will hear the recording twice.

Man: Hi Peter. I wanted to ask you something. Do you know when your summer holidays start?

Boy: It's the middle of June, about the 13th I think. Why?

Man: Well, you know when Mum goes on her painting course in France the week of the 16th . . . I've decided to go to Scotland.

Boy: Yeah?

Man: A friend of mine called Jim has asked if I want to go with him and spend a week camping there . . . we'll do lots of hill walking and climbing . . .

Boy: Sounds great. Go for it Dad! I suppose you want me to stay and look after the house, don't you?

Man: Well actually, I was wondering if you wanted to come with me . . . Jim has got a son your age, and he's coming too . . . I thought you might enjoy going off and doing a few things together . . . and it would be good to have a proper break before you start your summer job.

Boy: Oh, I see – that's a great idea Dad . . . I'd love to come . . . but I really don't have the money for a holiday.

Man: Well. It won't cost much. I'll drive us up to Scotland. The campsite belongs to a friend of Jim's, so that won't cost anything . . . and of course Jim and I will pay for food and drink and things like that.

Boy: In that case, I'd love to come. Have you ever met Jim's son?

Man: Oh yes, several times, when he was a bit younger.

Boy: What's he like?

Man: He's very similar to Jim – easy to get on with, enjoys sport and good food . . . I'm sure you'll find plenty to talk about.

Boy: Perhaps we could all get together some time soon . . . you know, have a chat and plan a few things . . .

Man: We could try, but it might be difficult. Jim's job takes him all over the world, but let's ask. Shall I phone him tonight?

Boy: Good idea. Catch you later, Dad.

Man: Okay then.

[pause]

Now listen again.

[The recording is repeated.]

That is the end of Part 4.

[pause]

You now have six minutes to check and copy your answers on to the answer sheet.

Note: Teacher, stop the recording here and time six minutes. Remind students when there is **one** minute remaining.

That is the end of the test.

Test 4

PAPER 1   READING AND WRITING

READING

Part 1

1 A   2 B   3 C   4 C   5 B

Part 2

6 C   7 B   8 F   9 E   10 G

Part 3

11 B   12 A   13 B   14 B   15 B   16 A   17 B   18 A   19 A
20 B

Part 4

21 C   22 B   23 D   24 A   25 D

Part 5

26 A   27 B   28 C   29 D   30 B   31 B   32 C   33 D   34 B
35 A

WRITING

Part 1

1 near/close to
2 are the
3 to put
4 so
5 cold as

Part 2

Task-specific Mark Scheme

The content elements that need to be covered are:

i   apology for missing the English class tomorrow
ii   reason why candidate cannot attend the class
iii suggestion of what candidate can do to cover the work missed

The following sample answers can be used as a guide when marking.

SAMPLE A (Test 4, Question 6: Note to a teacher)

> Dear teacher,
>
> I am going to miss the class tomorrow and I would like to tell you that I'm really sorry. I can't be there because I am going to the doctor at ten o'clock.
>
> I spoke yesterday with Carlie, she is going to me my work.

Examiner Comments

Points 1 and 2 are clearly dealt with, but point 3 is somewhat confused.

Mark: 4

SAMPLE B (Test 4, Question 6: Note to a teacher)

> Dear Mary
>
> I should apologise, I'm missing tomorrow's class, I can't be there because I'm ill.
>
> After 2 or 3 days I thing I'm OK.
>
> Could you do to cover the work by Franck.
>
> Thanks a lot
>
> Christian

Examiner Comments

All content elements are attempted, but the message requires some effort by the reader.

Mark: 3

SAMPLE C (Test 4, Question 6: Note to a teacher)

Dear Mr Dupont

I am sorry but I am going to miss the class tomorrow. I must go to the doctor at 9.00 a.m because I brocken my finger between the door and the sofa. Could you please give the work that I will miss to Julie who could give me it tomorrow at lunch.

Thank you in advance

Martine

Examiner Comments

Very good text – all points covered and clearly communicated to the reader.

Mark: 5

SAMPLE D (Test 4, Question 7: Letter to a penfriend)

Hi Barbara

I'm very glad to receive your letter. I didn't hear you for long time. When I saw you last time you prefer wearing red colour but I think it is good idea change your minght. Black trousers is more fashinable. What about me? I always go shopping when I am free although I haven't much money. I living in the close shopping centre where it is big sale for a smart clothes. Anyway I would like to invite you and enjoy together.

I look forward to seeing from you.

Bye

(signature)

Examiner Comments

This is an adequate attempt with ambitious but flawed language, e.g.: 'I think it is good idea change your minght'. There is an adequate range of structures and vocabulary, e.g.: 'Anyway I would like to invite you', 'smart clothes' and some linking of ideas with 'when' and 'but'. However, there are a number of errors, mostly non-impeding, e.g.: 'Black trousers is more fashinable'. Some effort is required from the reader.

Band: 3

SAMPLE E (Test 4, Question 7: Letter to a penfriend)

Hello Cheryl,

Thanks a lot for your lovely letter! I also like shopping for clothes but during the sales I never find my size! Usually, I like wearing jeans and jumpers and I often buy them in black since I really like this colour. My mother wanted to buy me some clothes for Christmas so I have been looking for some nice clothes for the last two weeks and I think I will ask her a blue polo-neck I saw in a shop last week. I hope you are feeling well.

Take care

XXX

(signature)

Examiner Comments

This is a very good attempt with confident and ambitious use of language. There is use of a wide range of structures and vocabulary within the task set, e.g.: 'I have been looking for some nice clothes for the last two weeks', 'polo-neck' and the narrative is well-organised and coherent through use of linking devices, e.g.: 'since', 'also'. There are very few errors and no effort is required from the reader.

Band: 5

SAMPLE F (Test 4, Question 7: Letter to a penfriend)

Hi Dear friend

I hope you are fine friend I am also fine. I bought a clothes last week becaus I found in supermarke I was looking very beutiful when I saw first time I really had a wish to buy and its colour is black and I told u befor black is my faverta colour and when I have been in the supermarke I saw a lots of clouthes but that was the only one I chose becaus I like to wear black dress you know any way Let me know how are you what about you what did you buy when you have been last time on shopping OK take care and rember me.

May you live long

(signature)

Examiner Comments

This is an inadequate attempt with unambitious language and an inadequate range of structure and vocabulary, e.g.: '. . . and its colour is black and I told u befor black is my faverta colour and . . .'. The absence of punctuation leads to some incoherence, e.g.: 'Let me know how are you what about you what did you buy when you have been last time on shopping . . .' and there are quite a few errors, mostly non-impeding, and in spelling, e.g.: 'faverta', 'clouthes', 'beutiful', 'befor'. Considerable effort is required from the reader.

Band: 2

SAMPLE G (Test 4, Question 8: The lost suitcase)

'The lost suitcase'
It was the last day of December. Everywhere was covered by snow. Rorry was waitting for train. He had to go to city and buy some medicine for his mother. Finally he jumped up to the train and set next to a serious man who left the train in the next station. Sudenly Rorry saw his suitcase which was left in the train. He didn't know what he should do. In the one hand he wanted to come back to his mother as soon as possible, on the other hand he felt responsibility for that suitcase. Finally he decided to caught the man and give him the suitcase. When he gave the suitcase to the man, he was so supprised because there were a lot of money and some important documents in that. So the man decided to give Rorry a reward and when he introduced himself, Rorry found that he was his mum's doctor. So he didn't had to city. He was so happy and asked the doctor to go to his home.

Examiner Comments

This is a good attempt with fairly ambitious use of language, e.g.: 'He felt responsibility for that suitcase . . .'. There is a more than adequate range of structures, e.g.: 'Rorry saw his suitcase which was left', 'give Rorry a reward' and a coherent narrative structure with some linking, e.g.: 'finally', 'on the other hand'. There are some errors, generally non-impeding, e.g.: 'Rorry was waitting', 'sudenly' and only a little effort is required from the reader.

Band: 4

SAMPLE H (Test 4, Question 8: The lost suitcase)

The lost suitcase

Tom was 18 years old he came to London to complet his study in Oxford college he met a girl from his cantry study with hem in the same course day after day the feel love with hear and he ask hear to be his girlfriend after for year Tom and his girlfriend went back to there cantry. Tom was cary three suitcase when they arrive in the earbort he didn't found The Thered suitcase. He get angry and start looking every where he foundet after one houre. We bring the same suitcase in his girlfriend bearthday and he oben the suitcase and give his girl frind a butiful driss for there widing.

Examiner Comments

This is an inadequate attempt as although the language may show signs of ambition, it is very flawed and frequently difficult to interpret, leading to incoherence. The numerous errors frequently impede communication, although there are a few comprehensible phrases, e.g.: '. . . met a girl from his cantry . . .'. The text requires considerable effort from the reader.

Band: 2

SAMPLE I (Test 4, Question 8: The lost suitcase)

> THE LOST SUITCASE
> THE HOUSE WAS CALM AND DARK WHEN MARK ARRIVED HOME
> HE WAS ON A SCHOOL TRIP TO SPAIN AND EVERYTHING SEEMED TO BE OKAY
> TILL THE MOMENT WHEN HE FOUND THAT HE HAD LOST HIS SUITCASE.
> HE WAS THINKING ABOUT WHAT TO SAY TO PARENTS ALL HIS WAY HOME,
> BUT HE DIDN'T DECIDE YET.
> AFTER FEW MINUTES THE DOOR WAS OPENED AGAIN. IT WAS HIS MUM WHO
> WAS ARRIVING.
> 'HI' SHE SAID. 'I WANTED SURPRISE YOU AND GIVE YOU A LIFT HOME FROM
> THE AIRPORT, BUT I COULDN'T FIND YOU ANYWHERE. THE ONLY THING I
> FOUND IS YOUR SUITCASE.'
> MARK WAS SO GLAD THAT HE STARTED SMILE AND WAS SMILING FOR NEXT
> TWENTY MINUTES.

Examiner Comments

This is a very good attempt with a confident and natural use of language and good use of direct speech. There is a wide range of structures, particularly tenses, e.g.: 'I COULDN'T FIND YOU ANYWHERE. THE ONLY THING I FOUND IS YOUR SUITCASE' and the narrative is coherent, with good use of simple linkers, e.g.: 'WHEN', 'TILL', 'AFTER'. The errors are minor and non-impeding, e.g.: 'I WANTED SURPRISE YOU' and articles, but no effort is required from the reader.

Band: 5

PAPER 2   LISTENING

Part 1

1 B   2 C   3 B   4 B   5 A   6 C   7 C

Part 2

8 B   9 A   10 C   11 A   12 B   13 C

Part 3

14   fit
15   rain
16   boots
17   mini-bus
18   March
19   01252 88492

Part 4

20 A   21 A   22 B   23 A   24 B   25 B

Test 4 transcript

This is the Cambridge Preliminary English Test, Test 4. There are four parts to the test. You will hear each part twice.

For each part of the test, there will be time for you to look through the questions and time for you to check your answers.

Write your answers on the question paper. You will have six minutes at the end of the test to copy your answers onto the answer sheet.

The recording will now be stopped. Please ask any questions now, because you must not speak during the test.

[pause]

Now open your question paper and look at Part 1.

PART 1　　*There are seven questions in this part. For each question there are three pictures and a short recording. Choose the correct picture and put a tick in the box below it.*

Before we start, here is an example.

Where did the man leave his camera?

Man:　　Oh no! I haven't got my camera!

Woman:　But you used it just now to take a photograph of the fountain.

Man:　　Oh I remember, I put it down on the steps while I put my coat on.

Woman:　Well, let's drive back quickly – it might still be there.

[pause]

The first picture is correct so there is a tick in box A.

Look at the three pictures for Question 1 now.

[pause]

Now we are ready to start. Listen carefully. You will hear each recording twice.

One. Which of Miranda's things will Lucy be able to use?

Woman:　Lucy's joining the tennis club, so that'll be more equipment I have to buy.

Man:　　Oh well, don't waste too much money. We bought Miranda everything, but then she only went once because she didn't like the teacher. Actually, I think we've still got some of it somewhere. There's a box of balls in the cupboard certainly, but she gave her cousin the racket, and she wears the shoes for other things. But I could look in the cupboard and give you what's there.

Woman:　Oh thanks, that'd be great. That would be really helpful.

[pause]

Now listen again.

[The recording is repeated.]

[pause]

Two. What can't the woman find?

Woman:　I'm going to mend and paint the shelves in your bedroom today.

Man:　　Great, Mum. Anything I can do to help?

Woman:　Yes, can you go to the shop and get me a new paint brush – this one's too old. But before you do that, ask your father what he's done with the hammer – I've looked everywhere for it. There was nothing in the toolbox except this pair of scissors which I lost months ago!

[pause]

Now listen again.

[The recording is repeated.]

[pause]

Three. Which ring has the woman lost?

Woman: I wonder if you can help me? I ate here in this restaurant last night, and I think I left my ring in the bathroom when I washed my hands. Have you seen it? It's got a square bluey-green stone with lots of smaller stones round it. It's quite valuable but that's not the point – it was my grandmother's and I'd hate to lose it.

[pause]

Now listen again.

[The recording is repeated.]

[pause]

Four. What time did the girl arrive?

Man: Sorry I'm late – have you been here long?

Woman: Well . . . not really, about five or ten minutes perhaps. I left home at five past six and got here at exactly quarter to seven.

Man: Well . . . if we hurry, we'll still make it for the beginning of the film at seven.

[pause]

Now listen again.

[The recording is repeated.]

[pause]

Five. What will be on television at 10 o'clock this evening?

Man: Here is an announcement about a change to our advertised programmes this evening. The football match between Spain and Hungary is now going to finish later than expected. When the match ends at 10.30 our programmes will continue as planned with a visit to an open air rock concert. But 'The Blue World' programme about life under the sea, which was due to begin at 10.00 o'clock this evening will now be shown next week instead.

[pause]

Now listen again.

[The recording is repeated.]

[pause]

Six. Where will the party be?

Man: What time are we leaving for Maria's party tonight?

Woman: Not too early. It'll only take ten minutes to get to the nightclub.

Man: Oh, I thought we were all meeting at the outdoor concert?

Woman: There's been a change of plan. The two of us are meeting Maria at the club. We've told her the party's there. But the other guests will go to her flat and prepare everything while we keep Maria busy. We'll take her back there after about an hour – she will be surprised!

[pause]

Now listen again.

[The recording is repeated.]

Key

[pause]

Seven. What did the man buy?

Woman: Oh, good, you're home! Did you get all the shopping? How about the orange juice?

Man: Well, actually, at first I thought the shop didn't have any orange juice. I was thinking we'd have to manage without. Then I realised they'd moved it to a different shelf. I hope this is enough.

Woman: Don't worry, that's plenty. Did you find the grapes?

Man: Yes, there were lots of grapes. Only they looked a bit sour, so I got strawberries instead. They were a bit expensive, though.

[pause]

Now listen again.

[The recording is repeated.]

That is the end of Part 1.

[pause]

PART 2   *Now turn to Part 2, questions 8–13.*

You will hear a man called Paul Hart talking about his trip to Africa with a team of scientists.

For each question, put a tick in the correct box. You now have 45 seconds to look at the questions for Part 2.

[pause]

Now we are ready to start. Listen carefully. You will hear the recording twice.

Woman: With us today, to tell us about his trip across Africa, is the biologist Paul Hart.

Man: We started on the east coast and travelled on foot across Africa to Gabon in the west, collecting plants and flowers along the way. It wasn't easy, but my route crossed a region rich in plants and I chose it because it won't stay that way for long when more roads are built. It was my only chance to get important information about the natural life of the area.

I had a team of eleven scientists. We walked from six in the morning, but the forest was so thick it took hours to cut our way through it, and some days we only walked one kilometre before dark. Fortunately, we carried special equipment that was very light and we took as little food as possible. But we were always tired when we put the tents up at night.

Sometimes we saw elephants or lions. They were amazing to watch and never attacked us. Every day, I collected plants and added to my notes. There was so much new information to write down. There were, of course, some low points, especially when I got anxious about the team. It was my job to make sure everyone got home safely.

Towards the end of the trip, I suddenly discovered one day that the food had nearly all gone. It was strange because we'd brought enough dried food with us to last the trip – food that wouldn't ever go bad – and we'd stopped at villages for fresh food too. But then I found that some of the team had eaten much more than they were supposed to. I was angry with them because it was a silly thing to do.

Then we started walking again. There were no maps for the area, but we had a local guide. Then one of the team got sick and we couldn't go any further. We let him rest, but he got much worse. Thankfully his life was saved by a fisherman who came along the river in a boat and took him to a doctor in the nearest village.

150

Finally, I returned home, and I'm back with my family and friends. I really missed them while I was away. But I learnt so much on the trip and I'm really glad I went. I was asked to go on another trip – this time to Australia – but I said that I couldn't because I'm busy here in London. And I think I've done enough travelling.

[pause]

Now listen again.

[The recording is repeated.]

That is the end of Part 2.

[pause]

PART 3   *Now turn to Part 3, questions 14–19.*

You will hear a woman talking about flights in a hot air balloon.

For each question, fill in the missing information in the numbered space. You now have 20 seconds to look at Part 3.

[pause]

Now we are ready to start. Listen carefully. You will hear the recording twice.

Woman: If you're looking for an extra special present for yourself or a friend, why not book a flight in a hot air balloon! These exciting trips give you the chance to enjoy a really unusual view of the countryside.

Children under 12 must be accompanied by an adult. There's no upper age limit and everyone is welcome. However, it is essential that all passengers are fit. This is because you will have to climb in and out of the basket under the balloon.

For a successful flight we need light winds. It's also important that there's no rain and that we have a clear sky. If there is too much cloud we'll cancel the flight and re-arrange it for another date.

The temperature in the air is similar to that on the ground so you should wear casual outdoor clothes. Also, you must remember to wear boots. That's because you may have to walk in fields that are wet and dirty at the end of the trip!

The direction the flight takes depends on the wind. The pilot will choose a suitable landing place which may be between 5 and 30 kilometres from the airfield we start from. But don't worry because transport is provided – a mini-bus will collect you. You won't have to walk all the way back to the airfield!

All our flights take place in the evening and departure times depend on when the sun sets. The season starts in March, and in May, for example, the flights would be at 6.00 p.m. The last flights are in October, and after that we close for the winter.

If you'd like to book a flight or to receive more information about hot air balloons, just call 01252, double 8, 492, or visit our website www.hotairballoons.com. It'll be a trip you'll never forget . . .

[pause]

Now listen again.

[The recording is repeated.]

That is the end of Part 3.

[pause]

PART 4   *Now turn to Part 4, questions 20–25.*

Look at the six sentences for this part. You will hear a conversation between a girl called Ella, and her father, about the school holidays.

Decide if each sentence is correct or incorrect. If it is correct, put a tick in the box under A for YES. If it is not correct, put a tick in the box under B for NO. You now have 20 seconds to look at the questions for Part 4.

[pause]

Now we are ready to start. Listen carefully. You will hear the recording twice.

Man: So Ella, the holidays at last! What are you going to do for the next three weeks?

Girl: Nothing, just relax. I've been so busy at school recently, what with my exams and everything; I just want to relax for a while.

Man: Well, yes you have done a lot of studying, but surely you want to do <u>something</u> in the holidays . . . I don't know . . . have some friends round perhaps or maybe we could all go camping for a few nights?

Girl: Mmm . . . I always have friends round in term time; I'd just like to have some time to myself.

Man: Oh, I see.

Girl: Anyway, to be honest, I need a break from my friends. All they ever do is talk about pop-stars and make-up. None of them seem to be interested in my kind of things.

Man: OK, then. How about you, your brother Alex and me going off to the beach for a couple of days; you know Alex loves camping and I could easily take some time off work . . .

Girl: Dad, it's spring! The sea will be freezing and there'll probably be a gale blowing, like last time, when we had to come home early because our tent got flooded! No way! I just want to relax in my warm, cosy bedroom thanks!

Man: Yes, but you need to get out and get some fresh air. I know . . . I thought you were going to help Mr Atkins with that new horse he's bought. What happened to that idea?

Girl: Well, I'd love to do that this holiday, but when I asked him about it he said that he thought I was perhaps too young to look after a horse on my own. "Maybe next year" he said.

Man: Well, I give up! Don't get to the end of the holiday and complain that you've been bored with just sitting around all the time! Nothing I suggest seems any good . . .

[pause]

Now listen again.

[The recording is repeated.]

That is the end of Part 4.

[pause]

You now have six minutes to check and copy your answers on to the answer sheet.

Note: Teacher, stop the recording here and time six minutes. Remind students when there is **one** minute remaining.

That is the end of the test.

UNIVERSITY *of* **CAMBRIDGE**
ESOL Examinations

 S A M P L E

Candidate Name	Centre No.
If not already printed, write name in CAPITALS and complete the Candidate No. grid (in pencil).	
Candidate Signature	**Candidate No.**
Examination Title	**Examination Details**
Centre	

Supervisor:

If the candidate is ABSENT or has WITHDRAWN shade here

0	0	0	0
1	1	1	1
2	2	2	2
3	3	3	3
4	4	4	4
5	5	5	5
6	6	6	6
7	7	7	7
8	8	8	8
9	9	9	9

PET Paper 1 Reading and Writing Candidate Answer Sheet 1

Instructions

Use a PENCIL (B or HB).

Rub out any answer you want to change with an eraser.

For **Reading:**
Mark ONE letter for each question.
For example, if you think **A** is the right answer to the
question, mark your answer sheet like this:

Part 1	**Part 2**	**Part 3**	**Part 4**	**Part 5**
1 A B C	6 A B C D E F G H	11 A B	21 A B C D	26 A B C D
2 A B C	7 A B C D E F G H	12 A B	22 A B C D	27 A B C D
3 A B C	8 A B C D E F G H	13 A B	23 A B C D	28 A B C D
4 A B C	9 A B C D E F G H	14 A B	24 A B C D	29 A B C D
5 A B C	10 A B C D E F G H	15 A B	25 A B C D	30 A B C D
		16 A B		31 A B C D
		17 A B		32 A B C D
		18 A B		33 A B C D
		19 A B		34 A B C D
		20 A B		35 A B C D

Continue on the other side of this sheet →

153

S A M P L E

For **Writing (Parts 1 and 2):**

Write your answers clearly in the spaces provided.

Part 1: Write your answers below.	Do not write here
1	1 1 0
2	1 2 0
3	1 3 0
4	1 4 0
5	1 5 0

Part 2 (Question 6): Write your answer below.

Put your answer to Writing Part 3 on Answer Sheet 2 ➜

Do not write below (Examiner use only)					
0	1	2	3	4	5

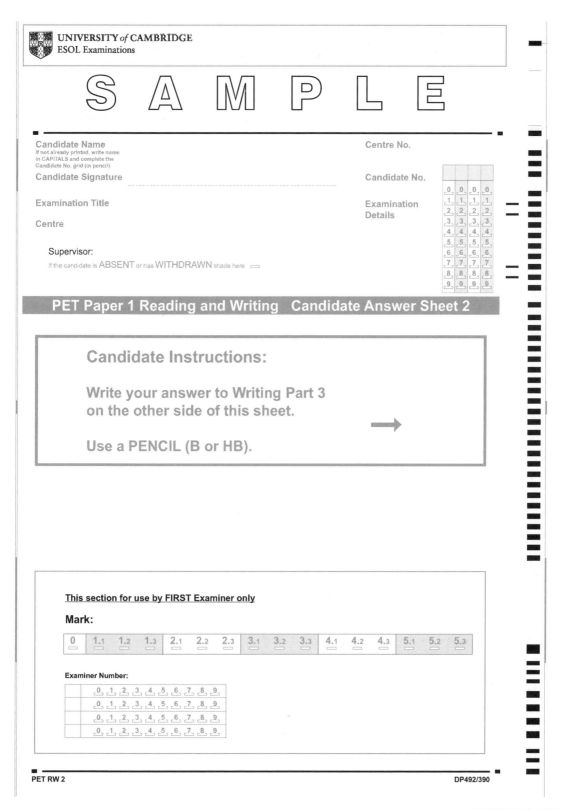

SAMPLE

Do not write below this line

This section for use by SECOND Examiner only

Mark:

0	1.1	1.2	1.3	2.1	2.2	2.3	3.1	3.2	3.3	4.1	4.2	4.3	5.1	5.2	5.3
⌣	⌣	⌣	⌣	⌣	⌣	⌣	⌣	⌣	⌣	⌣	⌣	⌣	⌣	⌣	⌣

Examiner Number:

	0 1 2 3 4 5 6 7 8 9
	0 1 2 3 4 5 6 7 8 9
	0 1 2 3 4 5 6 7 8 9
	0 1 2 3 4 5 6 7 8 9

UNIVERSITY *of* CAMBRIDGE
ESOL Examinations

S A M P L E

Candidate Name
If not already printed, write name in CAPITALS and complete the Candidate No. grid (in pencil).

Candidate Signature

Examination Title

Centre

Supervisor:
If the candidate is ABSENT or has WITHDRAWN shade here ▭

Centre No.

Candidate No.

Examination Details

0	0	0	0
1	1	1	1
2	2	2	2
3	3	3	3
4	4	4	4
5	5	5	5
6	6	6	6
7	7	7	7
8	8	8	8
9	9	9	9

PET Paper 2 Listening Candidate Answer Sheet

You must transfer all your answers from the Listening Question Paper to this answer sheet.

Instructions

Use a PENCIL (B or HB).

Rub out any answer you want to change with an eraser.

For **Parts 1, 2** and **4:**
Mark ONE letter for each question.
For example, if you think **A** is the right answer to the question, mark your answer sheet like this:

| 0 | A̶ B C |

For **Part 3:**
Write your answers clearly in the spaces next to the numbers (14 to 19) like this:

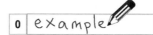

| 0 | example |

Part 1		Part 2		Part 3		Do not write here	Part 4	
1	A B C	**8**	A B C	**14**		1 14 0	**20**	A B
2	A B C	**9**	A B C	**15**		1 15 0	**21**	A B
3	A B C	**10**	A B C	**16**		1 16 0	**22**	A B
4	A B C	**11**	A B C	**17**		1 17 0	**23**	A B
5	A B C	**12**	A B C	**18**		1 18 0	**24**	A B
6	A B C	**13**	A B C	**19**		1 19 0	**25**	A B
7	A B C							

Answers

UNIVERSITY *of* **CAMBRIDGE**
ESOL Examinations

S A M P L E

Candidate Name
If not already printed, write name
in CAPITALS and complete the
Candidate No. grid (in pencil).

Centre No.

Candidate No.

Examination Title

**Examination
Details**

Centre

Supervisor:
If the candidate is ABSENT or has WITHDRAWN shade here ▭

0	0	0	0
1	1	1	1
2	2	2	2
3	3	3	3
4	4	4	4
5	5	5	5
6	6	6	6
7	7	7	7
8	8	8	8
9	9	9	9

PET Paper 3 Speaking Mark Sheet

Date of test:

Month   01 02 03 04 05 06 07 08 09 10 11 12

Day   01 02 03 04 05 06 07 08 09 10 11 12 13 14 15 16 17 18 19 20 21 22 23 24 25 26 27 28 29 30 31

Marks awarded:

Grammar and Vocabulary	0	1.0	1.5	2.0	2.5	3.0	3.5	4.0	4.5	5.0
Discourse Management	0	1.0	1.5	2.0	2.5	3.0	3.5	4.0	4.5	5.0
Pronunciation	0	1.0	1.5	2.0	2.5	3.0	3.5	4.0	4.5	5.0
Interactive Communication	0	1.0	1.5	2.0	2.5	3.0	3.5	4.0	4.5	5.0
Global Achievement	0	1.0	1.5	2.0	2.5	3.0	3.5	4.0	4.5	5.0

Test materials used: 1 2 3 4 5 6 7 8 9 10

Assessor's number	Interlocutor's number	Test format	Number of 2nd Candidate	Number of 3rd Candidate
A A 0 0 A A	A A 0 0 A A	Examiners : Candidates	0 0 0 0	0 0 0 0
B B 1 1 B B	B B 1 1 B B		1 1 1 1	1 1 1 1
C C 2 2 C C	C C 2 2 C C	2 : 2	2 2 2 2	2 2 2 2
D D 3 3 D D	D D 3 3 D D		3 3 3 3	3 3 3 3
E E 4 4 E E	E E 4 4 E E	2 : 3	4 4 4 4	4 4 4 4
F F 5 5 F F	F F 5 5 F F		5 5 5 5	5 5 5 5
G G 6 6 G G	G G 6 6 G G		6 6 6 6	6 6 6 6
H H 7 7 H H	H H 7 7 H H		7 7 7 7	7 7 7 7
J J 8 8 J J	J J 8 8 J J		8 8 8 8	8 8 8 8
K K 9 9 K K	K K 9 9 K K		9 9 9 9	9 9 9 9

PET S   DP383/332